advancing learning, changing lives

BTEC First
ICT Practitioners

STUDY GUIDE

A PEARSON COMPANY

BTEC First Study Guide:
ICT Practitioners

Published by:
Edexcel Limited
One90 High Holborn
London WC1V 7BH
www.edexcel.org.uk

Distributed by:
Pearson Education Limited
Edinburgh Gate
Harlow
Essex CM20 2JE

First published 2007
Third impression 2008
ISBN 978-1-84690-174-4
Project managed, designed and typeset by Bookcraft Ltd, Stroud, Gloucestershire
Printed in Malaysia (CTP-VVP)

Cover image © iStock

The Publisher's policy is to use paper manufactured from sustainable forests.

All reasonable efforts have been made to trace and contact original copyright owners.

Contents

Preface

Following a BTEC programme is an exciting way to study. It gives you the opportunity to develop the knowledge, skills and understanding that you will need in the world of work.

BTECs are very different from GCSEs; a BTEC puts *you* in charge of your own learning. This guide has been written specially for you, to help you get started and succeed on your BTEC First course.

The **introduction**, Your BTEC First, tells you about your new course. This will be your companion through the BTEC First, as it:

- tells you how your BTEC will differ from GCSE;

- suggests how you can plan your time;

- explains ways to make the most of visits, guest speakers and work experience;

- advises you about resources and how to find information;

- gives you advice on making presentations and doing assignments.

The **activities** give you tasks to do on your own, in small groups or as a class. You will have the opportunity to put into practice the theory you learn. The activities will help you prepare for assessment by practising your skills and showing you how much you know. These activities are *not* intended for assessment.

The sample **marked assignments** (also sometimes called marked assessments) show you what other students have done to gain a Pass, Merit or Distinction. By seeing what past students have done, you should be able to improve your own grade.

Your BTEC First will cover either three or six units, depending on whether you are doing a Certificate or a Diploma. In this guide the activities cover sections from three units: Unit 1 'Using ICT to Present Information', Unit 2 'Introduction to Computer Systems' and Unit 3 'ICT Project'. These units underpin your study of ICT Practitioners.

Because the guide covers only three units, it is important that you do all the other work your tutor sets you. Your tutor will ask you to research information in textbooks, in the library and on the internet. You may also have your own textbook for the course: use it! You should have the chance to visit local organisations or welcome guest speakers to your institution. This is a great way to find out more about your chosen vocational area – the type of jobs that are available and what the work is really like.

This guide is a taster, an introduction to your BTEC First. Use it as such, and make the most of the rich learning environment that your tutors will provide for you. Your BTEC First will give you an excellent base for further study, a broad understanding of ICT Practitioners and the knowledge you need to succeed in the world of work.

Your BTEC First

Starting a new course is often both exciting and scary. It's normally exciting to do something new, and this includes learning different subjects that appeal to you. BTEC First courses are work-related, so you will be focusing on the work area that interests you. It can be nerve-wracking, though, if you are worried that there may be some topics that you will not understand, if you are unsure how you will be assessed, or if the prospect of some aspects of the course – such as finding out information on your own, or giving a presentation – makes your blood run cold!

It may help to know that these are worries common to many new BTEC First students. Yet every year thousands of them thoroughly enjoy their courses and successfully achieve the award.

Some do this the easy way, while others find it harder.

The easy way involves two things:

*   knowing about the course and what you have to do

*   positive thinking

Knowledge of the course means that you focus your time and energy on the things that matter. Positive thinking means that you aren't defeated before you start. Your ability to do well is affected by what goes on in your mind. A positive attitude helps you to meet new challenges more easily.

This guide has been written to give you all the information you need to get the most out of your course, to help you to develop positive thinking skills, and, of course, to help you successfully achieve your award. Keep it nearby throughout your course and re-read the relevant parts whenever you need to.

DO THINK	DON'T THINK
I'm quite capable of doing well on this course. First I need to check what I know about it and what I don't – and to fill in the gaps.	*If I struggle a bit or don't like something then so what? I can always drop out if I can't cope.*

Knowing about your course

If a friend or relative asked about your course, what would you say? Would you just shrug or give a vague comment? Or could you give a short, accurate description? If you can do this it usually means that you have a better understanding of what your course is all about – which means you are likely to be better prepared and better organised. You are also more likely to make links between your course and the world around you. This means you can be alert to information that relates to the subject you are studying.

→ Your family, friends, or other people you know may talk about topics that you are covering in class.

→ There may be programmes on television which relate to your studies.

→ Items in the news may be relevant.

→ You may work in a part-time job. Even if your part-time work is in a different area, there will still be useful links. For example, for most BTEC First courses you need to know how to relate to other people at work, how to assist your customers or clients and how to communicate properly. These are skills you need in most part-time jobs.

If you have only a hazy idea about your course then it is sensible to re-read any information you have been given by your school or college and to check further details on the Edexcel website at www.edexcel.org.uk. At the very least, you should know:

• the type of BTEC award you are aiming for and how many units you will be taking:

◊ BTEC First Diploma – normally taken as a full-time course, with six units

◊ BTEC First Certificate – may be taken as a full-time or part-time course, with three units

• the titles of your core units and what they cover

• the number of specialist units you must take and the options available to you

Core units are compulsory for all students at all centres, and you can find details of them on the Edexcel website. The range of specialist units you can choose will depend upon which award you are taking and where you are studying. Many centres design their courses to meet the needs of the students in their area, in which case you won't have complete freedom to choose your own options. If you do have a choice, find out the content of each of the specialist units available, then think carefully about the ones you would most like to study. Then talk through your ideas with your tutor before you make a final decision.

DO THINK	DON'T THINK
The more I know about my course, the more I can link the different parts together and see how they relate to other areas of my life. This will give me a better understanding of the subjects I am studying.	*It's unlikely that any course will have much relevance to my life or my interests, no matter what anyone says.*

Knowing the difference: BTEC First versus GCSE

BTEC First awards are different from GCSEs in several ways. In addition to the differences in content, the way the topics are taught and the tutors' expectations of their students are also often different. Knowing about these gives you a better idea of what to expect – and how you should respond.

→   BTEC First awards are work-related. All the topics you learn relate to the skills and knowledge you will need in the workplace.

→   They are practical. You will learn how to apply your knowledge, both on your own and as a member of a team, to develop your skills and abilities.

→   Most full-time BTEC First Diploma courses in colleges are completed in one year. If you are taking a BTEC First Certificate course alongside your GCSEs, then you will probably be doing this over two years.

→   There are no exams. So you won't be expected to revise and learn lots of facts, or to write answers to questions in a hot exam room next June. Instead, you will complete assignments set by your tutors, based on learning outcomes set by Edexcel. You can read more about assignments on page 19, but for now you can think of them as being similar to coursework. They will be given to you through the year, and each will have a deadline. See page 19 for advice on coping with assignments, and page 9 for advice on managing your time effectively.

→   On a BTEC First course you will achieve Pass, Merit and Distinctions in your assignments. You will then be awarded an overall Pass, Merit or Distinction for the whole course.

→ BTEC First students are encouraged to take responsibility for their own learning. Your tutors won't expect to have to stand over you all the time to check what you are doing. This helps you to develop the skills to be mature and independent at work. You will be expected to be keen and interested enough to work hard without being continually monitored. You will also be expected to become more self-reliant and better organised as the course progresses. Some students thrive in this situation. They love having more freedom, and are keen to show that they can handle it, especially when they know that they can still ask for help or support when they need it. Other students – thankfully, a minority – aren't mature enough to cope in this situation, so it goes to their head and they run wild.

→ If you've just left school and are going to study for your BTEC First in a college, then you will find many other differences. No bells or uniforms! Maybe fewer timetabled hours; probably longer lesson periods. You will mix with a wider range of people, of different ages and nationalities. You are starting a whole new phase of your life, when you will meet new people and have new experiences. However strange it may seem at the beginning, new students normally settle down quickly. Even if they have been disappointed with some of their grades at GCSE, they are relieved that they can put this disappointment behind them and have a fresh start. If this applies to you, then it's up to you to make the most of it.

DO THINK	**DON'T THINK**
On my BTEC First course I can find out more about the area of work that interests me. I will enjoy proving that I can work just as well with less direct supervision, and know I can get help and support when I need it.	*Doing a BTEC First will be great because the tutors won't be breathing down my neck all the time and won't care if I mess around on the course.*

Knowing how to use your time

How well organised are you? Do you always plan in advance, find what you've put away, and remember what you've promised to do without being reminded? Or do you live for the moment – and never know what you will be doing more than six hours in advance? Would you forget who you were, some days, unless someone reminded you?

School teachers cope with young students like this by giving homework on set nights, setting close deadlines, and regularly reminding everyone when work is due. They don't (or daren't!) ask students to do something over the next couple of months and then just leave them to it.

Although your BTEC First tutor will give you reminders, he or she will also be preparing you for higher-level courses and for having a responsible job – when you will be expected to cope with a range of tasks and deadlines with few, if any, reminders. On your BTEC First course some work will need to be completed quickly and done for the next session. But other tasks may take some time to do – such as finding out information on a topic, or preparing a presentation. You may be set tasks like this several weeks in advance of the deadline, and it can be easy to put them off, or to forget them altogether – with the result that you may not do the task at all, or end up doing a sloppy job at the last minute because you haven't had time to do it properly.

This problem gets worse over time. At the start of a new course there always seems to be a lot of time and not much pressure: the major deadlines may seem far in the future, and you may find it easy to cope day by day.

This situation is unlikely to last. Some tasks may take you longer than you had thought. Several tutors may want work completed at the same time. And deadlines have a nasty habit of speeding up as they approach. If you have lots of personal commitments too, then you may struggle to cope, and get very stressed or be tempted to give up.

The best way to cope is to learn to manage your own time, rather than letting it manage you. The following tips may help.

→ Expect to have work to do at home, both during the week and at weekends, and plan time for this around your other commitments. It's unrealistic to think that you can complete the course without doing much at home.

→ Schedule fixed working times into your week, taking your other commitments into account. For example, if you always play five-a-side football on Monday evening, keep Tuesday evening free for catching up with work. Similarly, if you work every Saturday, keep some time free on Sunday for work you have to complete over the weekend.

→ Get into the habit of working at certain times, and tell other people in your life what you are doing. If you've no work to do on one of these days, then that's a bonus. It's always easier to find something to do when you unexpectedly have free time than to find time for a task you didn't expect.

→ Write down exactly what you have to do in a diary or notebook the moment you are told about it, so that you don't waste time doing the wrong thing – or ringing lots of people to find out if they know what it is you're supposed to be doing.

→ Normally you should do tasks in order of urgency – even if this means you can't start with the one you like the best. But if, for example, you need to send off for information and wait for it to arrive, you can use the time to work on less urgent tasks.

→ Don't forget to include in your schedule tasks that have to be done over a period of time. It's easy to forget these if you have lots of shorter deadlines to meet. Decide how long the whole task is likely to take you, break the total time up into manageable chunks, and allocate enough time to complete it by the deadline date.

→ Always allow more time than you think you will need, never less.

→ Be disciplined! Anyone who wants to get on in life has to learn that there are times when you have to work, even if you don't want to. Try rewarding yourself with a treat afterwards.

→ If you are struggling to motivate yourself, set yourself a shorter time limit and really focus on what you are doing to get the most out of the session. You may be so engrossed when the time is up that you want to carry on.

→ Speak to your tutor promptly if you have a clash of commitments or a personal problem that is causing you serious difficulties – or if you have truly forgotten an important deadline (then vow not to do so again)!

→ If few of these comments apply to you because you are well organised, hard-working and regularly burn the midnight oil trying to get everything right, then don't forget to build leisure time and relaxation into your schedule. And talk to your tutor if you find that you are getting stressed out because you are trying too hard to be perfect.

DO THINK	DON'T THINK
I am quite capable of planning and scheduling the work I have to do, and being self-disciplined about doing it. I don't need a tutor to do this for me.	*I can only work when I'm in the mood and it's up to my tutors to remind me what to do and when.*

Knowing about resources

Resources for your course include the handouts you are given by your tutor, the equipment and facilities at your school or college (such as the library and resource centre), and information you can obtain on the internet from websites that relate to your studies. Resources that are essential for your course – such as a computer and access to the internet – will always be provided. The same applies to specialist resources required for a particular subject. Other resources – such as paper, file folders and a pen – you will be expected to provide yourself.

→ Some popular (or expensive) resources may be shared, and may need to be reserved in advance. These may include popular textbooks in the library, and laptop computers for home use. If it's important to reserve this resource for a certain time, don't leave it till the last minute.

→ You can only benefit from a resource if you know how to use it properly. This applies, for example, to finding information in the library, or using PowerPoint to prepare a presentation. Always ask for help if you need it.

→ You cannot expect to work well if you are forever borrowing what you need. Check out the stationery and equipment you need to buy yourself, and do so before the course starts. Many stationers have discounts on stationery near the start of term.

→ Look after your resources, to avoid last-minute panics or crises. For example, file handouts promptly and in the right place, follow the guidelines for using your IT system, and replace items that are lost or have ceased to work.

DO THINK	DON'T THINK
I have all the resources I need for my course, and I know how to use them or how to find out.	*I can find out what's available if and when I need it, and I can always cadge stuff from someone else.*

Knowing how to get the most from work experience

On some BTEC First courses – such as Children's Care, Learning and Development – all students must undertake a related work placement. On others, work placements are recommended but not essential, or may be required only for some specialist units. So whether or not you spend time on work experience will depend upon several factors, including the course you are taking, the units you are studying, and the opportunities in your own area. You will need to check with your tutor to find out whether you will be going on a work placement as part of your course.

If you need evidence from a work placement for a particular unit, then your tutor will give you a log book or work diary, and will help you to prepare for the experience. You should also do your best to help yourself.

Your placement

→ Check you have all the information about the placement you need, such as the address, start time, and name of your placement supervisor.

→ Know the route from home and how long it will take you to get there.

→ Know what is suitable to wear, and what is not – and make sure all aspects of your appearance are appropriate to your job role.

→ Know any rules, regulations or guidelines that you must follow.

→ Check you know what to do if you have a problem during the placement, such as being too ill to go to work.

→ Talk to your tutor if you have any special personal worries or concerns.

→ Understand why you are going on the placement and how it relates to your course.

→ Know the units to which your evidence will apply.

→ Check the assessment criteria for the units and list the information and evidence you will need to obtain.

DO THINK	DON'T THINK
Work experience gives me the opportunity to find out more about possible future workplaces, and link my course to reality.	*Work experience just means I'll be given all the boring jobs to do.*

Knowing how to get the most from special events

BTEC First courses usually include several practical activities and special events. These make the work more interesting and varied, and give you the opportunity to find out information and develop your skills and knowledge in new situations. They may include visits to external venues, visits from specialist speakers, and team events.

Some students enjoy the chance to do something different, while others can't see the point. It will depend on whether or not you are prepared to take an active involvement in what is happening. You will normally obtain the most benefit if you make a few preparations beforehand.

→ Listen carefully when any visit outside school or college, or any arrangement for someone to visit you, is being described. Check you understand exactly why this has been organised and how it relates to your course.

→ Find out what you are expected to do, and any rules or guidelines you must follow, including any specific requirements related to your clothes or appearance.

→ Write down all the key details, such as the date, time, location, and names of those involved. Always allow ample time so that you arrive five minutes early for any special event, and are never late.

→ Your behaviour should be impeccable whenever you are on a visit or listening to a visiting speaker.

→ Check the information you will be expected to prepare or obtain. Often this will relate to a particular assignment, or help you understand a particular topic in more detail.

→ For an external visit, you may be expected to write an account of what you see or do, or to use what you learn to answer questions in an assignment. Remember to take a notebook and pen with you, so that you can make notes easily.

→ For an external speaker, you may be expected to prepare a list of questions as well as to make notes during the talk. Someone will also need to say 'thank you' afterwards on behalf of the group. If your class wants to tape the talk, it's polite to ask the speaker for permission first.

→ For a team event, you may be involved in planning and helping to allocate different team roles. You will be expected to participate positively in any discussions, to talk for some (but not all) of the time, and perhaps to volunteer for some jobs yourself.

→ Write up any notes you make during the event neatly as soon as possible afterwards – while you can still understand what you wrote!

DO THINK	DON'T THINK
I will get more out of external visits, visiting speakers and team events if I prepare in advance, and this will also help me to get good grades.	*Trips out and other events are just a good excuse to have a break and take it easy for bit.*

Knowing how to find out information

Many students who are asked to find out information find it difficult to do so effectively. If they are online, they often print out too much, or can't find what they want. Similarly, too many students drift aimlessly around a library rather than purposefully search for what they need.

Finding out information is a skill that you need to learn. You need to know where to look, how to recognise appropriate information, and when to stop looking in order to meet your deadline, as well as what to do with the information when you've found it.

The first thing to realise is that you will never be asked to find out information for no reason. Before you start, you need to know what you are looking for, why it is needed, where you can find it, and the deadline.

This means you target your search properly and start looking in the right place.

Researching in the library

→ Find out the order in which books are stored. This is normally explained to all students during their induction.

→ Know the other resources and facilities that are available in your library besides books – for example, CD-ROMs and journals.

→ Take enough change with you so that you can photocopy articles that you can't remove. Remember to write down the source of any article you photocopy.

→ If you need specific books or articles, and aren't sure where they will be, try to visit during a quiet time, when the librarian can give you help if you need it.

→ If you find two or three books which include the information you need, that's normally enough. Too many can be confusing.

→ Check quickly if a book contains the information you need by looking in the index for the key words and then checking you can understand the text. If you can't, then forget it and choose another. A book is only helpful to you if you can follow it.

Researching online

→ Use a good search engine to find relevant websites. Scroll down the first few pages of the search results and read the descriptions to see which sites seem to be the best.

→ Remember to read all parts of the screen to check what's available on a website, as menus may be at the foot of the page as well as at the top or on either side. Many large sites have a search facility or a site map which you can access if you are stuck.

→ Don't get distracted by irrelevant information. If your searches regularly lead nowhere, ask your IT resource staff for help.

→ Don't print out everything you read. Even if printouts are free, too much information is just confusing.

→ Bookmark sites you use regularly and find helpful.

Researching by asking other people

This doesn't mean asking someone else to do the work for you! It means finding out about a topic by asking an expert.

→ Think about the people you know who might be able to help you because they have knowledge or experience that would be useful.

→ Prepare in advance by thinking about the best questions to ask.

→ Then contact the person and (unless you know the person well) introduce yourself.

→ Explain politely and clearly why you need the information.

→ Ask your questions, but don't gabble or ask them too quickly.

→ Write notes, so that you don't forget what you are told. Put the name and title of the person, and the date, at the top of the first page.

→ Ask if you can contact the person again, in case there is anything you need to check. Write down their phone number or email address.

→ Remember to say 'thank you'.

Using your information

→ Keep all your information on a topic neatly in a labelled folder or file. If you think you might want to reuse the folder later, put the title on in pencil rather than ink.

→ Refresh your memory of the task by re-reading it before you start to sift the information. Then only select pages that are relevant to the question you have been asked. Put all the other paper away.

→ Remember that you will rarely just be asked to reproduce the information that you have obtained. You will need to make decisions about which parts are the most relevant and how you should use these. For example, if you have visited a sports facility to find out what is available, then you may have to explain which activities are targeted at certain groups of people. You would be expected to disregard information that didn't relate to that task. Or you may be asked to evaluate the facilities, in which case you would have to consider how well the centre met the needs of its users and how it could do better.

→ Never rewrite copied information and pretend they are your own words! This is plagiarism, which is a serious offence with severe penalties. You need to state the source of your material by including the name of the author or the web address – either in the text, or as part of a list at the end. Your tutor will show you how to do this if you are not sure.

→ Write a draft and then ask your tutor to confirm that you are on the right track. You can also check with your tutor if you are unsure whether or not to include certain types of information.

DO THINK	DON'T THINK
Researching can be fun, and practice makes perfect. If I'm struggling to find something or to know what to include, I'll ask for help. Then it will be easier next time.	*The more I find the better, because collecting or writing a lot always impresses people.*

Knowing how to make a presentation

Presentations are a common feature of many BTEC courses. Usually you will be asked to do a presentation as a member of a team. If the team works together and its members support each other then this is far less of an ordeal than it may first seem. The benefits are that you learn many skills, including how to be a team member, how to speak in public, and how to prepare visual aids (often using PowerPoint) – all of which are invaluable for your future career.

Many students get worried about the idea of standing up to speak in front of an audience. This is quite normal, and can even improve your performance if you know how to focus your anxieties productively!

Presentation tasks can be divided into three stages: the initial preparations, the organisation, and the delivery.

Preparation

→ Divide up the work of researching fairly among the team.

→ Bear in mind people's individual strengths and weaknesses and allow for these, so that you all gain from working as a team.

→ Work out how long each person must speak so that you don't exceed your time limit (either individually or as a team).

→ Agree on the type of visual aids that would be best, given your topic. Keeping things simple is often more effective than producing something elaborate that doesn't work properly.

→ Decide on any handouts that are required, prepare these and check them carefully.

→ Check you know when and where the presentation will be held and what you should wear.

→ Think in advance about any questions you may be asked, both individually and as a team.

Organisation

→ Decide who will start and how each person will be introduced. Sometimes the lead person introduces everyone; on other occasions people introduce themselves.

→ Decide the most logical order in which to speak, bearing in mind everyone's contribution and how it fits into the overall presentation.

→ Prepare prompt cards. It's easy to forget some of the things you want to say, so put your main points down in the right order on a prompt card. Never read from this! Instead, write clearly and neatly so that you can just glance down to check on your next point.

→ Check you have sufficient copies of any handouts, and that these are clear and easy to read.

→ Rehearse several times and check your timings.

→ Get your clothes ready the night before.

→ Arrive at the event in plenty of time so that you're not in a rush.

Delivery

→ Take a few deep breaths before you start, to calm your nerves.

→ Make eye contact with your audience, and smile.

→ Keep your head up.

→ Speak a little more slowly than usual.

→ Speak a little more loudly than usual – without shouting.

→ Answer any questions you are asked. If you don't know the answer, be honest – don't guess or waffle.

→ Offer to help a team member who is struggling to answer a question, if you know the answer.

DO THINK

If I am well prepared and organised then my presentation will be OK, even if I'm really scared. The audience will always make allowances for some nerves.

DON'T THINK

I'm confident about speaking in public so I don't have to bother preparing in advance.

Knowing the importance of assignments

All BTEC First students are assessed by means of assignments. Each assignment is designed to link to specific learning outcomes. Assignments let you demonstrate that you have the skills and knowledge to get a Pass, Merit or Distinction grade. At the end of your course, your assignment grades together determine the overall grade for your BTEC First Certificate or Diploma.

Each assignment you are given will comprise specific tasks. Many will involve you in obtaining information (see page 14) and then applying your new-found knowledge to produce a written piece of work. Alternatively, you may demonstrate your knowledge by giving a presentation or taking part in an activity.

To get a good grade, you must be able to produce a good response to assignments. To do so, you need to know the golden rules that apply to all assignments, then how to interpret your instructions to get the best grade you can.

The golden rules for assignments

→ Read your instructions carefully. Check that you understand everything, and ask your tutor for help if there is anything that puzzles or worries you.

→ Check that you know whether you have to do all the work on your own, or if you will have to do some as a member of a group. If you work as a team, you will always have to identify which parts are your own contribution.

→ Write down any verbal instructions you are given, including when your tutor is available to discuss your research or any drafts you have prepared.

→ Check you know the date of the final deadline and any penalties for not meeting this.

→ Make sure you know what to do if you have a serious personal problem and need an official extension. An example would be if you were ill and expected to be absent for some time.

→ Remember that copying someone else's work (plagiarism) is always a serious offence – and is easy for experienced tutors to spot. Your school or college will have strict rules which state the consequences of doing this. It is never worth the risk.

→ Schedule enough time for finding out the information and making your initial preparations – from planning a presentation to writing your first draft or preparing an activity.

→ Allow plenty of time between talking to your tutor about your plans, preparations and drafts and the final deadline.

Interpreting your instructions to get the best grade you can

→ Most assignments start with a command word – for example, 'describe', 'explain' or 'evaluate'. These words relate to the level of answer required. A higher level of response is required for a Merit grade than for a Pass, and a higher level still for a Distinction.

→ Students often fall short in an assignment because they do not realise the differences between these words and what they have to do in each case. The tables below show you what is usually required for each grade when you see a particular command word.

→ As you can see from the tables, to obtain a higher grade with a given command word (such as 'describe'), you usually need to give a more complex description or use your information in a different way. You can refer to the example answers to real assignments, and tutor comments, from page 57 onwards.

→ You can check the command words you are likely to see for each unit in the grading grid. It is sensible to read this carefully in advance, so that you know the evidence that you will have to present to obtain a Pass, Merit or Distinction grade.

→ Be prepared to amend, redraft or rethink your work following feedback from your tutor, so that you always produce work that you know is your best effort.

→ Learn how to record your achievement so that you can see your predicted overall grade. Your tutor will show you how to do this, using the Edexcel *Recording your Achievement* form for your subject.

The following tables show what is required to obtain a Pass, Merit and Distinction, for a range of different 'command words'. Generally speaking:

- To obtain a Pass grade, you must be able to show that you understand the key facts relating to a topic.

- To obtain a Merit grade, you must be able to show that, in addition to fulfilling the requirements for a Pass grade, you can also use your knowledge in a certain way.

- To obtain a Distinction grade, you must be able to show that, in addition to fulfilling the requirements for a Pass and a Merit grade, you can also apply your knowledge to a situation and give a reasoned opinion.

Obtaining a Pass

Complete...	Complete a form, diagram or drawing.
Demonstrate...	Show that you can do a particular activity.
Describe...	Give a clear, straightforward description which includes all the main points.
Identify...	Give all the basic facts which relate to a certain topic.
List...	Write a list of the main items (not sentences).
Name...	State the proper terms related to a drawing or diagram.
Outline...	Give all the main points, but without going into too much detail.
State...	Point out or list the main features.

Examples:

- *List the main features on your mobile phone.*

- *Describe the best way to greet a customer.*

- *Outline the procedures you follow to keep your computer system secure.*

Obtaining a Merit

Analyse...	Identify the factors that apply, and state how these are linked and how each of them relates to the topic.
Comment on...	Give your own opinions or views.
Compare... Contrast...	Identify the main factors relating to two or more items and point out the similarities and differences.
Competently use...	Take full account of information and feedback you have obtained to review or improve an activity.
Demonstrate...	Prove you can carry out a more complex activity.
Describe...	Give a full description including details of all the relevant features.
Explain...	Give logical reasons to support your views.
Justify...	Give reasons for the points you are making so that the reader knows what you are thinking.
Suggest...	Give your own ideas or thoughts.

Examples:

- *Explain why mobile phones are so popular.*
- *Describe the needs of four different types of customers.*
- *Suggest the type of procedures a business would need to introduce to keep its IT system secure.*

Obtaining a Distinction

Analyse...	Identify several relevant factors, show how they are linked, and explain the importance of each.
Compare... Contrast...	Identify the main factors in two or more situations, then explain the similarities and differences, and in some cases say which is best and why.
Demonstrate...	Prove that you can carry out a complex activity taking into account information you have obtained or received to adapt your original ideas.

Describe...	Give a comprehensive description which tells a story to the reader and shows that you can apply your knowledge and information correctly.
Evaluate...	Bring together all your information and make a judgement on the importance or success of something.
Explain...	Provide full details and reasons to support the arguments you are making.
Justify...	Give full reasons or evidence to support your opinion.
Recommend...	Weigh up all the evidence to come to a conclusion, with reasons, about what would be best.

Examples:

- *Evaluate the features and performance of your mobile phone.*

- *Analyse the role of customer service in contributing to an organisation's success.*

- *Justify the main features on the website of a large, successful organisation of your choice.*

DO THINK	**DON'T THINK**
Assignments give me the opportunity to demonstrate what I've learned. If I work steadily, take note of the feedback I get and ask for advice when I need it, there is no reason why I can't get a good grade.	*If I mess up a few assignments it isn't the end of the world. All teachers like to criticise stuff, and I only wanted a Pass anyway.*

Knowing what to do if you have a problem

If you are lucky, you will sail through your BTEC First with no major problems. Unfortunately, not every student is so lucky. Some may encounter personal difficulties or other issues that can seriously disrupt their work. If this happens to you, it's vitally important that you know what to do.

→   Check that you know who to talk to if you have a problem. Then check who you should see if that person happens to be away at the time.

→   Don't sit on a problem and worry about it. Talk to someone, in confidence, promptly.

→   Most schools and colleges have professional counselling staff you can see if you have a concern that you don't want to tell your tutor. They will never repeat anything you say to them without your permission.

→   If you have a serious complaint, it's a good idea to talk it over with one of your tutors before you do anything else. Schools and colleges have official procedures to cover important issues such as appeals about assignments and formal complaints, but it's usually sensible to try to resolve a problem informally first.

→   If your school or college has a serious complaint about you, it is likely to invoke its formal disciplinary procedures, and you should know what these are. If you have done something wrong or silly, remember that most people will have more respect for you if you are honest about it, admit where you went wrong and apologise promptly. Lying only makes matters worse.

→   Most students underestimate the ability of their tutors to help them in a crisis – and it's always easier to cope with a worry if you've shared it with someone.

DO THINK	DON'T THINK
My tutors are just as keen for me to do well as I am, and will do everything they can to help me if I have a problem.	*No one will believe I have a problem. Tutors just think it's an excuse to get out of working.*

Finally...

This introduction wasn't written just to give you another task to do! It was written to help you to do your best and get the most out of your course.

So don't just put it on one side and forget about it. Go back to it from time to time to remind yourself about how to approach your course. You may also find it helpful to show it to other people at home, so that they will understand more about your course and what you have to do.

Activities

1.1   Information types and sources

In this section we will focus on grading criterion P2 from Unit 1 'Using ICT to Present Information'.

Learning outcome

Understand the basis for selecting appropriate software to present and communicate information

Content

Information: finding information (ICT sources and non-ICT sources); checking validity of information

Grading criterion

P2: describe the different types and sources of information and ways of checking its validity

Activity 1

Make a list of all the different sources of information you can think of (not just ICT-based sources) in a table like the one below. For each source, list its format (e.g. electronic, written, visual, oral) and briefly describe the sort of information you can obtain from the source, with some examples.

Activity 2

Working in small groups, discuss how you can check the validity of each of the sources of information. Validity is to do with the correctness and accuracy of information. For example, you might ask someone at the bus stop what time the next bus comes, and they may give you an answer that is inaccurate, perhaps because the timetable has recently changed. You may read an article in a newspaper, but the person who wrote the article may not have researched it well and some of the things written in the article may be inaccurate. In some cases, information may be deliberately misleading.

Checking the validity of information can be as simple as asking someone else or checking with another source.

Add a column to the table you created in Activity 1, labelled 'How to check validity'. Then for each of the sources of information listed, enter the way you agreed in your group discussions that validity could be checked.

Activity 3

Still in small groups, discuss the consequences of using information that is inaccurate. In some situations the consequences may be fairly minor, but in other situations they may be more serious. For example, if you write an article in a newspaper about a person and some of the information is inaccurate or unfair, then you and the newspaper may be in serious trouble.

- Take a look at the Press Complaints Commission website (www.pcc.org.uk). What does this organisation do?
- Go to the BBC news website (http://news.bbc.co.uk) and search for 'libel'. Using the results of the search, find out what libel is and give some examples.

Research the consequences of inaccurate information, and report back your findings to the whole class.

Activity 4

In small groups, discuss the possible sources of information that could be used in each of these examples, how those sources could be validated, and the consequences of using inaccurate information.

1. planning a holiday
2. purchasing a spare part for a car
3. a doctor treating a rare disease
4. resolving a technical problem with the software on a computer
5. estimating the cost of constructing a new building

Source of information	Format	Sort of information, with examples

Activity 5

Task 1

Wikipedia is an online encyclopaedia (www. wikipedia.org) that is written and updated by volunteers from around the world. However, there have been a number of controversies over the qualifications of the people who update the entries and the validity of the information included in them. Search for Wikipedia on the BBC news website to read some articles about these problems.

- What problems have occurred with the validity of information on Wikipedia?
- How were they resolved?
- Why is it important that the information on Wikipeida be accurate?

Task 2

You can also read about how articles are written for Wikipedia by going to the site and clicking the 'About' link, which appears on every article page (not the front page), then reading section 3 'Contributing to Wikipedia'. Also search on Wikipedia for 'reliability of wikipedia' to read an article about how articles are submitted and about several studies on the reliability of information on Wikipedia and other encyclopaedias.

What have the articles written in the *Guardian* and *Nature* revealed about the accuracy of Wikipedia?

1.2   Types of document

In this section we will focus on grading criterion P1 from Unit 1 'Using ICT to Present Information'.

Learning outcome

Understand the purpose of different document types

Content

Types of document: short formal eg memo, email, letter, order form, invoice, agenda, minutes; extended formal eg article, newsletter, report, user guide; graphical document eg illustrations, charts, flowcharts, diagrams; promotional eg advertisement, leaflet, web page; presentation; informal documents eg texting, creative writing

Grading criterion

P1: describe the structure and purpose of different documents, one from each document type

Activity 1

In order to identify the structure or layout of different document types, you need to collect a reasonable number (perhaps two or three) of examples of each type listed in the 'Content' for this Unit. Some should be fairly easy for you to collect examples of (such as a web page, a magazine or newspaper article, a leaflet and an advertisement). Your tutor/teacher should be able to help you find some types of documents (such as memos, agenda and minutes).

Sort your collection of documents according to the overall types (short formal, extended formal, graphical, promotional, informal), and then complete a table like the one below.

Type: short formal	
Document	Purpose

Type: extended formal	
Document	Purpose

Type: graphical	
Document	Purpose

Type: promotional	
Document	Purpose

Type: informal	
Document	Purpose

In small groups, compare the different examples you have found and try to identify common elements within each type. For example, what do all your formal documents have in common?

Activity 2

This activity will help you identify the general structure of each type of document. Use the collection of documents you have put together for Activity 1. Make a standard form on which to record the following information for each type of document:

- document type
- length (single page or multi-page)
- structure (fixed or variable)
- graphical content, if any
- whether single-subject or many-subject
- whether divided into sections
- other features (e.g. headers or footers, page numbers, index, table of contents)
- whether usually presented on paper or electronically

Activity 3

Traditionally, business letters have had a fixed structure, although these days it isn't always followed. The traditional layout is as shown below.

Look at the business letters your have collected. Do they follow this layout, or are they different? Do any of the other documents you have collected have a fixed structure? If so, describe it.

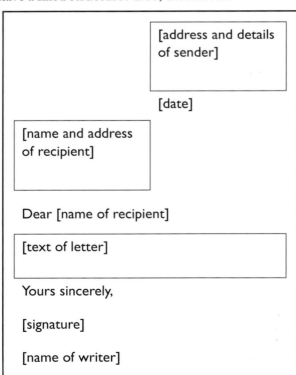

1.3 Audience types

In this section we will focus on grading criteria P3, M1, M2 and D2 from Unit 1 'Using ICT to Present Information'.

Learning outcome

Understand the purpose of different document types

Content

Audience types: eg commercial customers, individual adults, internal staff, children

Appropriate communication: meeting user need eg language, writing style; specialist tools eg readability tests; netiquette; summaries; templates; appropriate choice of application package

Grading criteria

P3: create documents making use of basic tools and techniques, one from each document type, that meet the need of a defined audience

M1: create different types of documents to convey the same information to different audiences

M2: create a complex document that combines textual, numerical and graphical information appropriate for a defined audience

D2: review a complex document and justify choice of tools and techniques in terms of the effectiveness of communication to the defined audience

Activity 1

Take a look at the four documents shown on page 29, and think about why they may not communicate very effectively with the audience they are aimed at.

Recommend ways in which these documents could be made more appropriate for their purpose.

Activity 2

The 'Content' specification for this Unit lists four different audience types, but this list can probably be extended. Working in small groups, create an

Parking ticket!

Yes, you have received a parking ticket!
What a silly thing to do, park where its not allowed! Never mind, just pay the £100 fine and everything will be OK!

Off season Senior Citizen Cruises
If you over 60 then you can come on one of our special low priced Caribbean cruises. These off season cruises are special designed for senior citizens and your every need will be catered for. The 7 night cruise starts with a flight to Miami from Gatwick or Manchester airport. You then join the luxury cruise ship SS Sun Valley for you cruise around the islands of the Caribbean.
Don't miss this opportunity of a lifetime, book now by phoning 0208 999777. You will need to pay a deposit of £200 then the remaining £400 4 weeks before you travel. Departure dates are 12 Feb, 21 Feb, 5th March and 19th March.

Develop your spoken English
Specially designed courses for people for whom English is not their native tongue.

Using proven pedagogical principals backed by the latest research into non-native language developmental techniques our intensive courses using intuitive and learner centred techniques will help you develop at a rapid pace.

To book call now on 01582 77788

After school club

Come and have fun at our after school club. For children aged 7 to 11. Runs form 3:30 to 6:30 Monday to Thursday

Lots of interesting exciting activities including artwork, games, story time and craft work.

Contact Mrs Smith in room 12A for more information

extended list with at least six types, taking into account age and background.

Using your new extended list, look at each of the documents you collected for the previous section and decide what the main target audience was for the document.

You may find that some of the audience types do not have any of the documents you collected aimed at them. If this is the case, try to find a document that is aimed at that audience.

For each of the audience types you have identified, list the features that documents aimed at that audience should have. An example table is shown below, with one audience type already entered.

Audience type	Document features
young children (3–6 years)	very simple, clear language colourful and interesting not too much text illustrative pictures

Activity 3

Task 1

Microsoft Word provides readability statistics as part of its grammar checker. To see the statistics on any document, choose the 'Tools' menu, then select 'Spelling and Grammar' and go through the document with the checker. When it has finished checking, it will display the readability statistics for the document. An example is shown below.

Choose a number of Word documents you have written (perhaps assignment work you have

previously done) – the documents need to be of a reasonable length, at least half a page – and try the readability tests on them. You could also try the tests on other documents, such as assignment briefs or the course handbook.

The statistics by themselves do not mean very much. Generally, the more words in a sentence, the harder it is to read, and using longer words (more characters per word) makes reading difficult. The Flesch Reading Ease and Flesh–Kincaid Grade Level are explained in the Word help pages. Search for 'readability' and then follow the link to 'Readability scores'.

Readability Statistics

Counts	
Words	11173
Characters	55865
Paragraphs	483
Sentences	506

Averages	
Sentences per Paragraph	2.6
Words per Sentence	18.6
Characters per Word	4.8

Readability	
Passive Sentences	33%
Flesch Reading Ease	46.7
Flesch-Kincaid Grade Level	11.3

OK

Task 2

Working in small groups, find a paragraph of text in one of the documents suggested in Task 1 that you find hard to read, select the text in Word, run the grammar checker to see the readability statistics on that paragraph, and note the results. Now try to revise the paragraph to make it easier to understand (for example, splitting long sentences into shorter ones and replacing long words with simpler short words with a similar meaning). Run the grammar checker again and see if the readability has improved.

Activity 4

'Netiquette' is a general term that refers to what is considered to be polite and respectful behaviour when using various forms of electronic (usually internet) communications, such as chatrooms, forums and e-mail. What is acceptable behaviour varies depending on the nature of the communications, so what is acceptable in a chatroom might not be so in a business e-mail! Some forums and chat services have a moderator who keeps an eye on the communication, and failure to follow the netiquette may result in expulsion from the chatroom or forum.

Discuss in small groups how netiquette applies in different circumstances. For example:

- How is the netiquette different for a business e-mail and a personal e-mail?

- Some of you may have joined web forums, as there are many of them around, covering almost every subject imaginable. Do you know what the netiquette rules are? They are sometimes listed under the heading 'FAQ' or 'Rules'.

- Have you ever been thrown out of a chatroom or forum by the moderator? What netiquette rules did you break?

- Why is it important to have netiquette rules? What purpose do they serve?

1.4   Selecting software

In this section we will focus on grading criteria P4 and D1 from Unit 1 'Using ICT to Present Information'.

Learning outcome

Understand the basis for selecting appropriate software to present and communicate information

Content

Applications for presenting and communicating information: text based (text editors, word processors); graphics software (graphic tools in packages, standalone graphic packages); presentation software; other technologies eg texting on mobile phones, e-mail, multimedia

Features: interface eg WIMP, GUI; voice recognition and voice output options; integrated packages; variety of outputs eg audience notes, speakers' notes, different file formats; automated procedures eg wizards; short cuts; use of templates; mail merge

Grading criteria

P4: select and use document templates

D1: create document templates using two different applications

Activity 1

You and a couple of your friends have decided to set up a charity to raise money for providing computers to schools in developing countries. Like any business, it will need stationery, including letterhead paper, order forms, invoice forms, memos, etc. You will also be going around schools and colleges giving PowerPoint presentations on the charity and raising funds.

Task 1

Design templates for all the documents, and the presentation slides that will display all the relevant information about the charity (name, address, contact details, etc.) along with a suitable logo and colour scheme.

Task 2

Discuss in small groups the following questions.

- What are the benefits and drawbacks of using templates?
- In a company with many employees, what difficulties might using templates create?
- What is a 'house style', and how do templates help in creating one?

Write down the answers to each question agreed by your group; then feed back your answers to the whole class.

Activity 2

Many application programs have a large selection of features. For example, a word processor such as Microsoft Word is not limited to creating letters and reports – you can also create graphics, tables, and complex documents that combine these elements. So which application is best for a particular purpose? In a table like the one below, enter the features of each type of software that makes it the best choice for its primary purpose.

1.5   Tools and techniques

In this section we will focus on grading criteria P3 and M3 from Unit 1 'Using ICT to Present Information'.

Learning outcome

Be able to use commonly available tools and techniques in application packages

Content

Formatting and editing tools: formatting text eg characters, paragraphs, pages; editing text eg insert, edit, delete; formatting graphics eg basic shapes, images, charts, tables; editing graphics eg draw, resize, align, rotate, flip; use of copy and paste; inserting special characters; advanced tools eg crop, paste special, arrange, paragraph styles, animation, tracking; combining information

Presentation techniques: choice of font and size; use of colour; different layouts eg columns, tables; headers and footers, styles; titles and headings; use of bullets; graphic images; advanced techniques eg tables of contents, indexes; speaker notes

Information storage: files; file details (name, size, type, date modified); file management eg naming files, folder structures, moving and deleting files

Type of program	Primary purpose	Features that support its primary purpose
word processing	production of documents (letters, reports, etc.)	
spreadsheet	numerical and financial calculations	
database	organisation of data	
presentation	creation of presentation slides	
graphics	creation of images	
desktop publishing	creation of documents with complex layout	

Grading criteria

P3: create documents making use of basic tools and techniques, one from each document type, that meet the needs of a defined audience

M3: use advanced formatting tools and techniques to enhance the presentation of information

Activity 1

Microsoft Office Online provides interactive training sessions, which can help you build your skills in using some of the advanced features of the Office products. To use these training sessions, first go to the Office Online website (http://office. microsoft.com). Then click the 'Help and How-to' tab at the top of the page (see screenshots below).

Then go to the 'Training' page and scroll to the bottom. Click the 'Office 2003' tab and then click on a product name (e.g. 'Word 2003').

You will then see a list of 30 or so training courses (see screenshot on page 34).

Each training course lasts about 30–40 minutes, and includes audio, so you will need headphones.

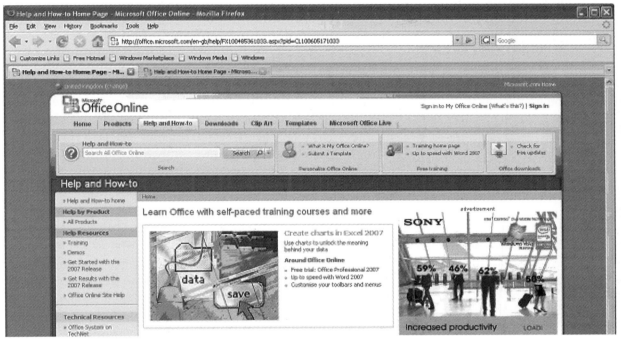

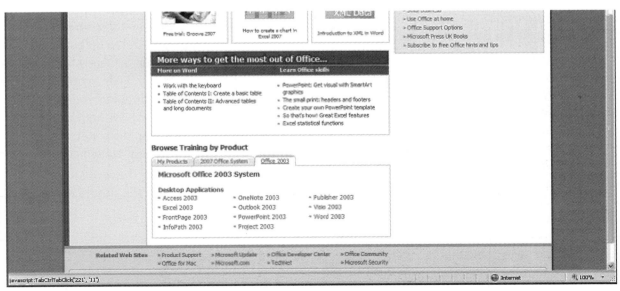

Depending on your existing skills and knowledge of Word, you might find the following ones useful:

- *Add graphics and keep them where you want them*
- *Tables I: Create and format basic tables*
- *Tables II: Use tables to simplify complex page layouts*
- *Table of Contents I: Create a basic TOC*
- *Headers and footers, simple to elaborate*
- *Format your document with styles*

There are also courses for PowerPoint and other Office products.

Activity 2

The following text has been typed without any formatting at all.

Changing a tyre

Changing a type can be tricky and for many people the best bet may be to call a motoring organisation such as the AA or RAC. However if you have reasonable mechanical skill you should be able to perform the task. The first thing you must do is gather the correct tools. You will need the following: a jack or other lifting device. A wheel brace or wrench of the correct size. A block to chock the wheels. It is very important indeed that you take proper safety precautions. Make sure the following precautions have been taken. The car must be on level ground, jacking up the car while on a slope is very dangerous. Never place any part of your body under a car which is supported only by a jack. You can only jack up a car on firm ground, if the ground is soft the jack will sink into it. To change the tyre follow these steps. Step 1. Make sure the handbrake is on. Step 2. Using the wheel brace loosen but don't remove the wheel nuts from the wheel you are changing. Step 3. Place the block under one of the wheels you are not removing to prevent the car from moving when you jack it up. Step 4. Find the jacking point next to the wheel you are removing, it should be close to the wheel arch towards the centre of the car. Engage the jack with the jacking point (check in your owner's manual). Step 5. Jack up the car. Step 6. Remove the wheel nuts and the wheel. Replace with the spare wheel. Step 7. Do up but don't fully tighten the wheel nuts. Step 6. Gently lower the car and remove the jack. Step 7. Fully tighten the wheel nuts. If you are in any doubt about your ability to complete this procedure, call for help. Wheel nuts are often very tight and you many not be able to remove them without special equipment.

Highlight the text to show the formatting you would apply to each part. You should at least use:

- bold text
- different fonts and sizes
- bullet points
- paragraph spacing

1.6   Reviewing documents

In this section we will focus on grading criteria P6 and D2 from Unit 1 'Using ICT to Present Information'.

Learning outcome

Be able to review and adjust finished documents

Content

Review: use of media; quality eg proof-reading, accuracy, functionality, aesthetics, spellchecking, grammar checking, thesaurus; feedback from other people; user requirements check; explaining decisions and actions taken eg choice of packages, choice of techniques and tools, layout

Grading criteria

P6: review and check documents

D2: review a complex document and justify choice of tools and techniques in terms of the effectiveness of communication to the defined audience

Activity 1

Using a spellchecker is only one way to check your documents, and it certainly won't guarantee they are correct. The following text does not contain any errors that a spellchecker would highlight (although a grammar check will spot some of them), but nonetheless it is full of errors. See if you can spot them all.

Keeping a dog

Dogs can be very rewarding pets but your should not underestimate the commitment involved in owing a dog. Puppies must be traced carefully as a disobedient dog can be very difficult to life with an dangerous. A dog should come when called and obey a range of other commands such as 'sit' and 'stop'. puppies will also need house training and this can be frustrating not to mention the unpleasant job of cleaning up then mess.

What breed of dog should you choose. This is important as different breed have different temperaments so you need to think about what kind of dog you want and consider issues such as how much exercise you will be able to give the door and if you have children in the house. Also consider how much time the dog will spend on its own in the hose.

Dogs can also be quite expansive to keep as well as buying food for them vets bills can be very expensive and you many want to consider assurance to cover the cost.

A well behaved dog is a please to own, they are loyal, affectionate and good company. However you need careful consider the commitment awning a dog required, as in the word of the famous slogan, 'a dog is not just for Christmas, its for life'.

Circle all the errors you can find. (There are at least 19.)

Activity 2

Task 1

Take a look at the PowerPoint slides on pages 36–37, and highlight all the formatting errors you can find.

Task 2

Wendy made quite a mess of her slideshow. Can you list a set of simple rules for creating PowerPoint slides that will help avoid these problems in the future?

My Summer
Holiday

WENDY Smith

We went to Portugal

- It was very hot

The beaches were very nice

**The country side was also very
pretty**

- The food was different

What we saw

- Lots of beautiful views
- Nice flowers

Slide 3

Our Villa

■ Our villa had a swimming pool

I hope you
enjoyed my slide
show

The end

2.1   Types of computers

In this section we will focus on grading criterion P1 from Unit 2 'Introduction to Computer Systems'.

Learning outcome

Know different uses of computers in homes and businesses

Content

Types of computers: PC (base unit, monitor, keyboard, mouse); server; embedded devices eg inside phones, washing machines, cars, games consoles, other eg mainframe, PDA

Users: home/commercial end users and IT practitioners eg software and website developers, administrators, help desk workers and technicians; types of tasks that users might perform on a computer; level of technical expertise users might need

Grading criterion

P1: describe the purpose of different types of computer

Activity 1

Working in small groups, make a list of all the different types of computer you can think of. You could use a table like the one below. You need to consider both personal computers and other devices and pieces of equipment that contain computers – sometimes called embedded computers. In this case a 'computer' can be any electronic device that takes input, carries out processing, can store data, and produces an output.

Add to your list a brief description of the purpose of the computer, and create a table like the one shown above (with an example). See the Unit 'Content' specification for examples of categories.

Activity 2

People use computers for all sorts of things, but we can broadly divide users into a number of types:

- home end users
- commercial end users
- IT practitioners

IT practitioners include people such as software and website developers, computer administrators, helpdesk workers and technicians.

Working in small groups, discuss what sort of tasks these different users might typically carry out on a computer and what level of technical expertise each of these groups of users might need. Then complete a table like the one at the top of page 39. In the 'Level of expertise' column, enter one of the following:

- little technical expertise required
- specialist expertise in a particular area required
- broad range of technical knowledge required

Activity 3

What skills and qualifications do IT practitioners need in the real world? One way to get an idea of this is to look at job adverts. These can also be a little misleading, as you will find that most jobs advertised require high levels of skill; this is because these sorts of jobs are harder to fill, whereas IT jobs with lower skills requirements (e.g. junior technicians) are much easier to fill and so don't need to be advertised so widely. Bear this in mind when looking at job adverts, and think of some of the jobs as longer-term aspirations rather than short-term aims.

The aim of this activity is to list the most common skills and qualifications seen in job adverts for the main types of IT practitioner jobs. There are a large number of websites that advertise jobs. The following are just a small selection:

- www.computingcareers.co.uk – mainly programmer and web-developer jobs

Type of computer	Purpose	Category
desktop PC	general purpose, runs a variety of software (e.g. business applications, games, entertainment)	PC

Type of user	Typical tasks	Level of expertise

- www.monster.co.uk – wide range of jobs
- www.totaljobs.com – reasonable range of IT jobs
- www.jobcenterplus.co.uk –follow the 'Job Search' link

Using the job categories listed in the table below, survey a range of jobs (preferably about ten) in each category and see which skills and qualifications get mentioned in at least three of the jobs you look at. This should give a reasonable idea of which skills and qualifications are most popular.

Once you have completed the table, work in small groups of three or four to compare the results you have found, and agree a combined list of the most important skills and qualifications.

2.2   User interfaces

In this section we will focus on grading criteria P2 and M1 from Unit 2 'Introduction to Computer Systems'.

Learning outcome

Know different uses of computers in homes and businesses

Content

User interface: command line operating system eg MS-DOS, Linux; Graphical User Interface (GUI) eg Microsoft Windows; specialised eg voice controlled; advantages and disadvantages of different types

Grading criteria

P2: describe how a command line and GUI operating system can perform the same task

M1: explain circumstances when it is more efficient to use a command line interface rather than a GUI interface

Activity 1

In this activity you will compare the use of operating-system commands with the command-line DOS system and the Windows GUI.

Perform the tasks in the table at the top of page 40.

Job category	Popular skills (e.g. teamwork, problem solving)	Popular qualifications (e.g. GCSEs, degree)
IT technician		
IT helpdesk		
programmer		
web developer		
computer administrator		
network administrator (or technician)		
IT support		

Task	DOS	Windows
List the contents of the 'My Documents' folder (assuming you are already in that folder).	Type: `dir`	Select 'My Documents' from the 'Start' menu.

Rename a file called 'myfile.doc' to 'yourfile.doc'.	Type:
	`rename myfile.doc`
	`yourfile.doc`
		Using Windows Explorer, either right-click on the file, choose 'Rename', and enter the new name; or click on the file, choose the 'File' menu, select 'Rename', and enter the new name.

Copy a file called 'yourfile.doc' from 'My Documents' to a folder called 'C:\test' (assuming you are already in that folder).	Type:
	`copy yourfile.doc`
	`C:\test`
		Right-click on the file, choose 'Copy', open 'My Computer', double-click on the 'C:' drive, double-click on the 'test' folder, right-click and choose 'Paste'. (You can also use the 'Edit' menu rather than right-clicking.)

List the contents of the 'My Documents' folder (assuming you are not already in that folder).	Type:
	`cd c:\Documents`
	`and Settings`
	`cd [current user]`
	`cd My Documents`
	`dir`
		Select 'My Documents' from the 'Start' menu.

Activity 2

In small groups, discuss the advantages and disadvantages of GUI and command-line user interfaces. You should consider these in relation to both the user and the hardware resources required. Complete a table like the one below, showing the outcome of your discussions.

2.3   Data flow and representation

In this section we will focus on grading criterion P3 from Unit 2 'Introduction to Computer Systems'.

Learning outcome

Be able to explain the use of common types of hardware in a personal computer system

	GUI		Command line	
	Advantages	Disadvantages	Advantages	Disadvantages
Inexperienced user				
Experienced user				
Hardware resources				

Content

Data representation: binary; bits and multiples eg megabytes, gigabytes

Grading criterion

P3: describe a standalone personal computer (PC) and show how data flows around the system

Activity 1

Imagine using a computer with word-processing software to type a simple letter. For each of the stages in this process as shown below, draw the main data flows between the system components.

Activity 2

ASCII (American Standard Code for Information Interchange) is a code that is used to represent characters (letters, numerals, etc.) in numeric form. Ultimately, inside the computer ASCII codes are stored as binary numbers, but the table below shows the decimal equivalents for the letters of the alphabet.

A	65	N	78	a	97	n	110
B	66	O	79	b	98	o	111
C	67	P	80	c	99	p	112
D	68	Q	81	d	100	q	113
E	69	R	82	e	101	r	114
F	70	S	83	f	102	s	115
G	71	T	84	g	103	t	116
H	72	U	85	h	104	u	117
I	73	V	86	i	105	v	118
J	74	W	87	j	106	w	119
K	75	X	88	k	107	x	120
L	76	Y	89	l	108	y	121
M	77	Z	90	m	109	z	122

Stage 1 – launch word-processing software

Stage 3 – save document

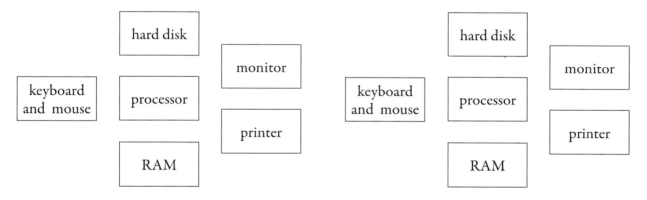

Stage 2 – type text into document

Stage 4 – print document

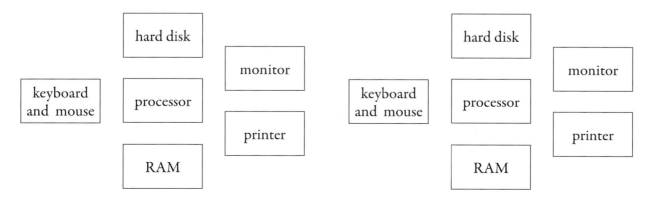

For example, 'BTEC' would be coded as 66 84 69 67. The space character is coded as 32.

Try coding:

1. your name

2. the name of your school or college

Numerals are represented by codes too: 'o' is 48, '1' is 49, and so on up to '9' which is '57'. So '10 High Street' would be:

49 48 32 72 105 103 104 32 83 116 114 101 101 116

Try coding your entire address, including the postcode.

The original ASCII code provided only 127 different characters; it was later extended to 256 characters. You can see the complete ASCII table at www.asciitable.com. Why were additional characters needed? ASCII is not used so much now, as the 256-character limit is rather restricting; instead, a code called Unicode is used. Research, using the internet, what Unicode is and how it differs from ASCII.

2.4   Hardware

In this section we will focus on grading criteria P4, M2 and D1 from Unit 2 'Introduction to Computer Systems'.

Learning outcome

Be able to explain the use of common types of hardware in a personal computer system

Content

Hardware: processor speed and type; memory eg RAM, cache; storage devices eg hard disk drive, floppy drive, CD ROM, flash drive, DVD; input devices eg graphics tablet, microphone, mouse, keyboard; output devices eg printer, monitor; modems eg dialup, broadband; network interface cards; costs

Performance: characteristics of component eg processor speed and type; data transmission speeds

Grading criteria

P4: specify suitable hardware and application software to meet a given user need

M2: justify choice of hardware and software to meet a given user need

D1: evaluate two possible computer systems (hardware and software) that meet a given user need in terms of both performance and value for money

Activity 1

Identify the name and purpose of each of the hardware items shown on pages 44–45. Write your answers in the boxes beside the pictures.

Activity 2

How can the performance of different computers be rated and compared? Computer magazines such as *PC Pro* and *Personal Computer World* often run 'group tests' where they test a number of similar computers from different makers. You can view some of these reviews online (www.pcw.co.uk and www.pcpro.co.uk – on the *PC Pro* website they are known as 'lab tests'), and download performance graphs. In these reviews, the performance levels of the computers are normally rated and compared using 'benchmark' programs.

Take a look at some of these reviews (preferably at least two), from different magazines; then answer the following questions. (You will generally find more information in the magazine than on the website.)

- What is a benchmark program?
- Why use a benchmark program?
- Which benchmark programs are used in the articles you have looked at?
- Why are several different benchmarks used? Why do they give different results?

Discuss in small groups what other ways you could use to measure the performance of a computer. Can you think of a way you could compare the performance of a computer at your college or school with that of one you have at home, without using benchmark software?

Activity 3

How is the performance of individual computer components rated? The two main measures are speed and capacity, but what are the actual units used, and what are the typical speed and capacity

Component	Units used to measure speed	Units used to measure capacity	Typical current speed	Typical current capacity
CPU				
memory				
graphics card				
sound card				
network card				
hard disk				
USB 'pen' drive				
CD writer				

of current PC components? Find out the answers to these questions and complete the table above.

2.5   Selecting software

In this section we will focus on grading criteria P4, M2 and D1 from Unit 2 'Introduction to Computer Systems'.

Learning outcome

Know how to select software for a specified user

Content

Systems software: operating systems; systems software tools eg diagnostic tools, file managers, disk utilities

Applications software: features of office applications software eg word-processing, spreadsheets, database, graphics, presentation and communication; games software; communications eg web browser; other software eg Computer Aided Design (CAD), programming languages, web development tools, route planning, voice recognition, speech synthesis; bespoke software

Compatibility: hardware and software

Grading criteria

P4: specify suitable hardware and application software to meet a given user need

M2: justify choice of hardware and software to meet a given user need

D1: evaluate two possible computer systems (hardware and software) that meet a given user need in terms of both performance and value for money

Activity 1

In small groups, make a list of all the different types of software you can think of. Using a table like the following, classify all the types you come up with, entering the group (e.g. office applications, utilities, entertainment, development, communications) and for each one giving an example of an actual software product and a brief explanation of what it is used for. One row has been completed as an example.

Type	Group	Example	Use
word processing	office	Microsoft Word	creating documents, letters, reports, etc.

Activity 2

Microsoft's new operating system, Windows Vista, comes in a number of different versions: 'Home Basic', 'Home Premium', 'Ultimate', 'Business' and 'Enterprise'. Using a table like the one on page 46, identify the difference between the versions. In the 'Main features' column, just list those features not included in other versions.

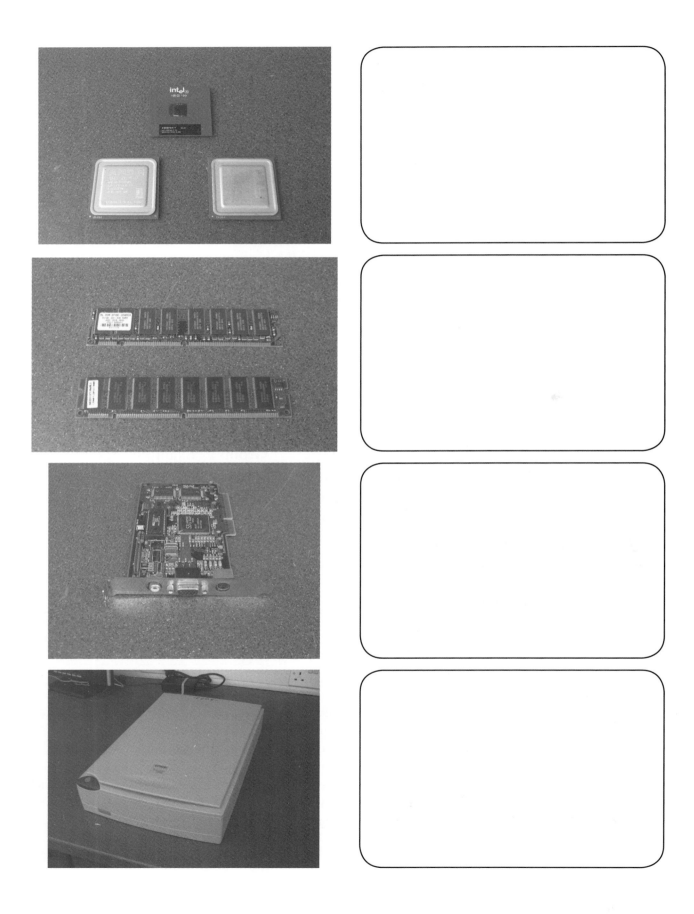

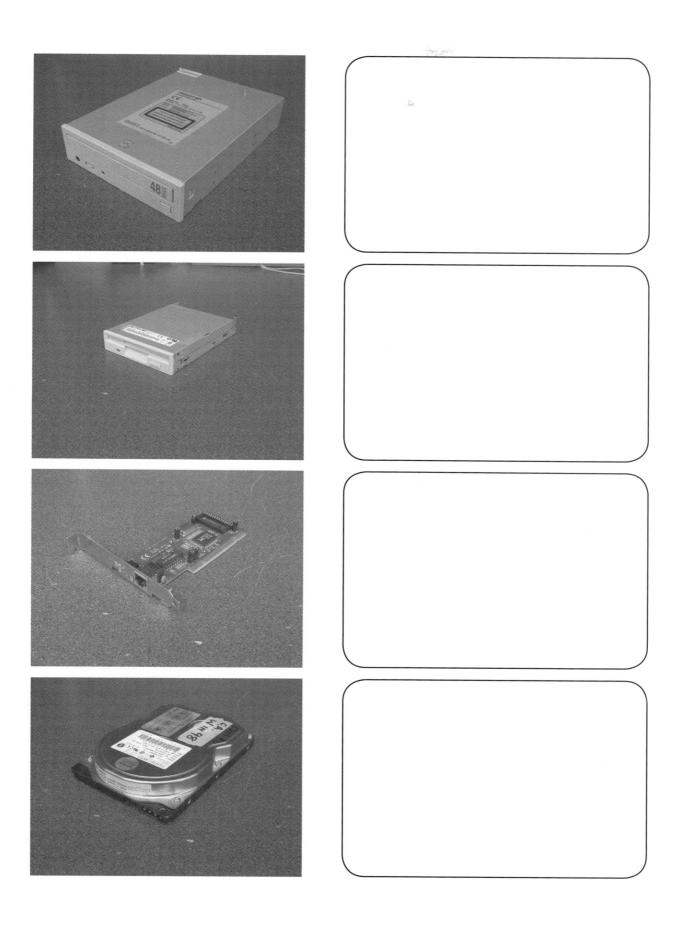

Version	Main features	Typical user	Price
Home Basic			
Home Premium			
Ultimate			
Business			
Enterprise			

The Linux operating system is a popular alternative to Windows. Carry out some research and try to identify the key differences between Windows and Linux. Linux is also available in many different versions, such as Mandrake, Ubuntu, Red Hat, etc. Research the differences between these versions.

2.6   Hardware connections

In this section we will focus on grading criterion P5 from Unit 2 'Introduction to Computer Systems'.

Learning outcome

Be able to safely connect hardware devices and configure software for a specified user

Content

Health and safety: electrical hazards; manual handling, impact on users eg RSI, eyestrain

Hardware connections: connection of peripheral devices to a PC system unit eg speakers, digital camera, scanner, web cam, barcode reader, graphics tablet, appropriate cabling; testing functionality

Grading criterion

P5: safely connect and test at least two peripherals to a personal computer

Activity 1

The top picture on page 47 shows the rear of a computer, with the different ports and connectors numbered.

Identify which cable in the bottom picture is attached to which port on the back of the computer.

Cable	Port no.	Purpose
A		
B		
C		
D		
E		
F		

Some of the ports shown on the back of the computer don't correspond to a cable shown in the picture. Which are they, and what are they for?

Activity 2

Health and safety are important for both computer users and computer technicians. Create a booklet, to be given to learners during the course induction, that explains the importance of health and safety, the issues that relate to both computer users and technicians, and the precautions that should be taken to minimise the risks. Use pictures and diagrams to illustrate the booklet. Make sure you cover the following issues:

- eye strain
- RSI
- electrical hazards
- workshop safety, including use of tools
- manual handling

To accompany the booklet, create a series of posters, for display in classrooms and computer workshops, reminding learners of the health and safety issues.

2.7   Software configuration

In this section we will focus on grading criteria P6 and M3 from Unit 2 'Introduction to Computer Systems'.

Learning outcome

Be able to safely connect and use hardware devices and configure software for a specified user

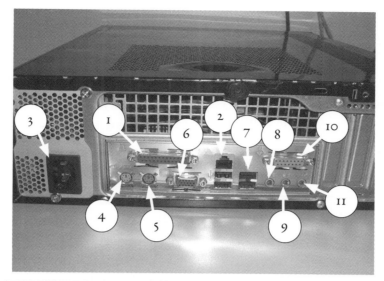

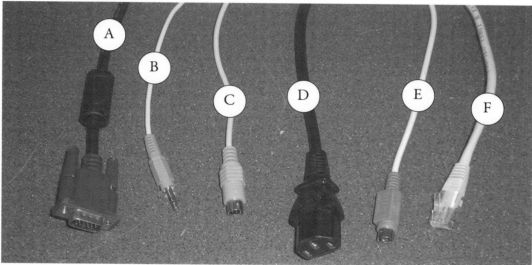

Content

Configuration of software: configuration to user requirement; personalising GUI operating system interface eg toolbar, shortcuts, taskbar, date/time, screen saver, mouse; folder structures; accessing data; user feedback

Grading criteria

P6: configure defined software for a given user need

M3: explain how the configuration of software will help a given user perform their tasks

Activity 1

You have been asked to help configure the Windows operating system to assist two users with special needs.

- One has impaired vision and finds it difficult to see the mouse pointer. They also need items on the desktop to be made larger than the standard size so that they can easily see them.
- The other person has limited manual dexterity. They cannot easily press multiple key combinations (such as CTRL+ALT+DELETE), and find it difficult to move the mouse.

Investigate what configuration options there are in Windows to help meet the needs of these two different users. Create a brief pictorial guide showing how the configuration options you identify can be set.

You can find more about Windows accessibility features using the Windows help pages: search for 'accessibility options'. You can also go to the RNIB website (www.rnib.org.uk) and search for 'accessibility features'.

Make a list of the accessibility options, and how they can be used to help people with disabilities, using a table like the following.

Accessibility option	What it does	Kind of disability it can help

Activity 2

There are many ways to configure and customise the Windows interface. Using a table like the one below, list the methods you can use to customise each one of the listed interface items, and list the customisations you can do. If you don't know which desktop item the name refers to, or how to customise it, search for the name in Windows help (under the 'Start' menu, 'Help and Support' option).

Interface item	How to customise	Possible customisations
'Start' menu		
taskbar		
notification area		
desktop		
screensaver		
'Quick Launch' bar		

2.8   Security

In this section we will focus on grading criteria P7, M4, D2 and D3 from Unit 2 'Introduction to Computer Systems'.

Learning outcome

Be able to safely connect hardware devices and configure software for a specified user

Content

System security: threats to data stored on a computer eg viruses, spyware, data theft, hacking, media failure; relevant and current legislation eg Data Protection Act 1998, Computer Misuse Act 1990; virus checking; backup procedures; firewalls; physical security; damage to equipment

Grading criteria

P7: list the possible data security and legal issues when using a computer in a given situation

M4: describe how hardware, software and data can be protected from potential threats

D2: evaluate current threats to the security of data stored in computer systems

D3: recommend measures in a given situation that will protect the commercial systems and comply with legal requirements

Activity 1

Thousands of viruses have been created, although many are rarely seen. Some viruses are very common. Research the following list of viruses, completing a table like the one below by entering the operating system (OS) each one affects, how it spreads and what it does.

Name	OS	How it spreads	What it does
Hckpk			
Netsky			
Zafi			
Sality			
MyDoom			
Bagle			
Clagger			

These viruses were common in February 2007, but new viruses come out all the time. Find out what the most commonly seen ones are at the moment by visiting www.sophos.com/security/top-10

Activity 2

The world of computer security uses a complex array of strange-sounding technical terms, but it is important to know what they mean. Create a glossary with definitions for all the computer-security-related terms listed on page 49. Don't simply copy and paste definitions from internet sites, but visit a number of sites with definitions so that you can develop an understanding of the term and write a simple definition in your own words.

You can use websites such as:

- www.wikipedia.org
- www.howstuffworks.com

The websites of companies that make virus protection software are also a good source of information:

- www.sophos.com
- www.grisoft.com
- www.mcafee.com

Write down definitions for the terms below:

- *phishing*
- *spam*
- *worm*
- *spyware*
- *trojan*
- *adware*
- *DOS attack*
- *mousetrapping*
- *page-jacking*
- *ransomware*
- *rootkit*
- *spoofing*
- *zombies*

3.1   What is a project?

In this section we will focus on grading criteria P1 and M4 from Unit 3 'ICT Project'.

Learning outcome

Understand use of models and activities involved in projects and some key factors that influence them

Content

Models: simple models eg plan-do-review

Factors that influence projects: internal and external factors; resource requirements eg money, hardware, software; timescales

Activities: outline proposal and justification; consider alternatives; gather information; produce project plan, gain permission to proceed; design and produce solution; monitor progress; testing and fixing of problems; user acceptance; maintenance

Gathering information: use of appropriate techniques eg questionnaires, observation, interviews, market research; checking for possible defects in information

Grading criteria

P1: explain factors that influence projects, giving examples

M4: describe with examples, problems that could arise if a project is not well planned

Activity 1

This activity prepares you for your project. It involves brainstorming and researching the nature and purpose of a project.

Task 1

In small groups, brainstorm the question: 'What is a project?' Have a flipchart or some paper ready, and then write down every idea that people in the group come up with. Here are some supplementary questions that may help you:

- Is a project different from any other assignment? If so, how?
- How is a project different from your day-to-day work?

Using the results of your brainstorming, create a definition of what a project is, then share and compare it with those of other groups.

A definition of a project from Wikipedia is as follows:

A project is a temporary endeavor undertaken to create a unique product or service.

How does that compare with your definition?

Task 2

Project management is a major subject in its own right, and over the years a number of models and techniques have been developed to plan and manage a project. It is worth looking at some of these, as they may be useful in planning and managing your own project. Research these project-management tools and find out what they involve:

- Gantt charts
- work breakdown structure
- PERT
- plan–do–review

Do you think any of these methods could help you plan and run your project?

Task 3

What activities are involved in running a project? Run a brainstorming session on this question and then produce an agreed list. Don't forget to cover the whole life-cycle of the project.

Task 4

Projects need resources. They also have constraints (things that limit how much of a certain resource a project is able to use). For example, your project will have a completion (or hand-in) date. This (and the fact that you have to sleep and do other work!) will constrain the amount of time you have available to complete the project. Once again, run a group brainstorming session thinking about what resources a project might need. (As you probably don't have an actual project in mind yet, you will have to be fairly general about the resources. The details will come later, when you have chosen your project and begin planning it.)

Activity 2

Choosing your project is a very important step. You need to select a project that gives you sufficient opportunity to demonstrate your skills, but you also need to select a realistic project that can be achieved using the time and resources available. Beware of choosing something too difficult: generally, the technically simpler the project is, the better. Remember, this Unit is not about demonstrating technical skill; it is about demonstrating your project planning and management skills.

You need to think up some project ideas, and then bring these to a group review session so that your fellow learners can help you decide. You will need to work in small groups, and present your ideas to

each other. Your fellow learners should ask you the following questions about your project idea:

- Is there a clearly defined user need? The project you do must meet some user need or requirement. It would be best if this was a real user, but an imaginary user can be used if someone can provide the information and feedback that a real user would provide.
- What resources are required? You should revisit the list of general resources you made in Activity 1, and now add detail, defining exactly what will be required. If any of the resources are not currently available you will need to say how they can be acquired.
- Do you have the technical skills to complete this project? If there are any skills you lack, you will have to say how you will acquire them.
- Is the project realistically achievable in the time available? This is the 'crunch' question. If you decide it is not possible, you will have to modify what you have in mind or think of something different for your project.

Activity 3

Wembley football stadium was one of the biggest construction projects in the UK at the time. The idea of a new 'home for English football' got off the ground in 1995, and it was thought that the project would take about four years to complete and cost £400 million. Construction began in 2001, and the plan was to have the stadium ready for the World Athletics Championships in 2005. In fact, the project cost is estimated to be around £1000 million, and it was not completed until March 2007. The company that built the stadium, Australian construction firm Multiplex, face a huge loss on the contract, as they agreed a fixed price at the outset. They have also suffered a big dent in their reputation.

Research the problems at the new Wembley stadium, using the internet, magazines and newspapers, and try to find some answers to the questions below.

- What went wrong? Why did the stadium take so much longer to construct than originally planned?
- What were the consequences of the project running so late? Some of the consequences to

Multiplex are mentioned above, but there are other consequences?

- The problems of the Wembley stadium raised concerns about another even bigger construction project, the 2012 London Olympics. This project must be ready when the Olympics start in July 2012. How is the project going? Is it on track? You can visit the London Olympics website (www.london2012.org) to find out more.

Activity 4

To carry out a project that meets some user needs, you will have to gather information about those needs. How will you collect this information for your project? This partly depends on who the users are, and if there is just one of them or a whole group. For example, suppose your project was to create a database of music tracks, and the users were going to be your fellow learners. How would you find out what their needs were? Some methods are:

- questionnaires
- observation
- interviews
- market research

Task 1

What do these methods involve, and what are the advantages and disadvantages of each? In small groups, discuss the answers to these questions, and complete a table like the one below.

Method	What it involves	Advantages	Disadvantages
question-naires			
observa-tion			
interviews			
market research			

Task 2

Research the answers to the following questions.

- What is market research? Why might you need to do market research? How could you do it?
- Designing and creating a questionnaire is a complex process. What makes a good questionnaire (and a bad one)?

3.2   How to plan a project

In this section we will focus on grading criterion P3 from Unit 3 'ICT Project'.

Learning outcome

Be able to identify requirements for a particular project, gather relevant information as required and create a project plan

Content

Requirements: purpose of project; why a solution is needed; who is it for; usability; inputs and outputs; processes; timescale, documentation; constraints

Usability: ease of use; access and disability issues; interfaces eg WIMP, voice

Project plan: ordered lists of activities; timescales; resources eg staffing, money, hardware, software

Grading criterion

P3: produce a project plan

Activity 1

'Why am I doing this project?' This might sound like a simple question, but it is important. A project needs to have a purpose. You need to ask questions like:

- *What is the purpose of the project?*
- *What problem will my project solve? Do I have a detailed description of the problem?*
- *Who are the users? What level of expertise do they have in using computers?*

Even if the users and the problem are not real, you will need answers to these questions, so you will need to use a realistic case study, perhaps based on a real situation that you are familiar with.

If the users and problem are real, you will need a way to capture this information, perhaps by meeting them and interviewing them, or by asking them to complete a questionnaire.

Activity 2

To make your project plan, you need to take the list of project activities you created in the last section (Activity 1 Task 3). Now sort your activities into chronological order (i.e. the activity you do first is first on the list, and so on). You may also be able to refine your list of activities (add to it, remove items, add more details) now that you know what your project is going to be. Make sure you have left nothing out.

Place the activities in a table with headings as in the example below. This project is to create a spreadsheet for a friend who owns a newsagents. He has a computer but is not very good at using it. He wants to create a spreadsheet to keep track of all his newspaper deliveries. The plan is not complete: it only shows the first few activities.

Of course, your project has a fixed completion (hand-in) date, so like the 2012 Olympics project it must be completed on time. Another way to plan your project is to complete the task plan in reverse order, starting with its completion. This way you can work back and find out when you must start.

Try completing another project-plan table, working backwards from the hand-in date.

If you discover you should have started some time ago, then your project is too complex to be completed within the time available, and you will have to re-think it.

Activity 3

Task 1

One of the most difficult aspects of planning is estimating how much time it will take you to do the various tasks. People often underestimate how long it takes to do something, and it may be difficult to estimate anyway if you haven't done that type of task before. You also have to take into account that things can go wrong: for example, you can be off sick, delaying the project by a couple of days. There are a number of ways you can try to get a better estimate of how long a task will take:

- How long did it take last time you did this (if you have done it before)?

- If you have never done a task like this before, try to find someone who has done something similar and ask them how long they think it will take.

- Build 'contingency' into your plan. This is additional time included to allow for problems and delays.

Stage	Name	Description	Duration	Elapsed time	Resources needed
1	investigation	Meet Mr Smith and discuss requirements.	1 day	1 day	bus fare
2	writing proposal	List what the system will do.	2 days	3 days	computer, MS Word
3	presenting proposal	Meet Mr Smith again and go through proposal with him; obtain approval.	1 day	4 days	bus fare
4	detailed design	Create design for the spreadsheet, including layout, input, output and formulae.	3 days	7 days	computer, MS Word, Excel

Review your plan with one of your fellow learners and see if they agree with your estimates; you can then review their plan. Ask each other questions to check that the tasks have been thought about carefully and you have included some contingency.

Task 2

As well as planning the tasks that will make up your project, you can also add project milestones. A milestone is an important point in your project. Unlike a task, which has a start and end date (and therefore a duration), a milestone is planned to occur on a particular date. For example, you might have various tasks that make up your research into the user requirements for the project, which culminate in you presenting a proposal to your users. At the end of this phase of the project you might add a milestone ('project proposal agreed with user'), which would have a particular date when it should be achieved. It is useful to add milestones to your project plan, as they help you monitor progress, and they also give you a sense of achievement as you pass each one. Typically you might have five or six milestones in your project, one of which will, of course, be the completion and hand-in of the project. Look at the plan you have been working on for Activity 2 and Task 1 of this activity, and see if you can add at least five milestones. Since milestones have dates rather than durations you will have to add dates to your plan.

Activity 4

What kind of user interface will your project have? Will the intended users find it easy to use? The designer and creator of an interface is often not the best person to judge how easy it is to use. (Why not?) One way you can test the usability of an interface is to create a prototype and then show it to the users. (If the users for your project are not real, then you can use anyone with a similar IT skill level as your imaginary users.) A prototype is a simple version of your interface, which does not need to work fully; in fact it could just be a neat hand-drawn sketch of the intended layout.

You can show your users the interface prototype and then note the comments they make about it and see if they feel it will be easy to use. It is very likely that they will have ideas about how it can be improved, or they will find things confusing or difficult to understand that you can easily improve on: for example, by adding to or improving the text or instructions that form part of the interface.

3.3   Monitoring the project

In this section we will focus on grading criteria P5 and M3 from Unit 3 'ICT Project'.

Learning outcome

Be able to execute a project and monitor progress within identified resources and timescales

Content

Monitor progress: work logs; update reports; interim testing

Timescales: milestones; interim reviews; handover date

Grading criteria

P5: monitor the progress of a project against a project plan

M3: monitor a project to completion against a project plan within identified timescales, producing interim reviews

Activity 1

Sometimes when doing a project there is a tendency to concentrate on the outcome – the final product. Of course, that is very important in real life, but in this Unit the process you go through to produce the product is equally, if not more, important. Most of the grading criteria for this Unit are about planning, monitoring and reviewing the project, so it is important that you put a lot of thought and effort into these areas. To help you provide evidence for these criteria, you should keep a *project diary* or work log. If you concentrate too much on doing the project, and leave the write-up to the end, you may forget things that happened day by day. Each day, or every couple of days, make an entry in the diary listing what you have done on your project, what problems you have come across, any changes you have made to your project plan or design, and so on.

A diary can also provide evidence for your interim reviews, which you must do to achieve M3. The diary is probably best kept electronically, although a paper-based one will do fine. You could create a blog (web log) and share your experiences and thoughts with your fellow learners. If you do this, you could support each other with ideas and suggestions to deal with problems you have come across.

Activity 2

How can you do an interim review? The two most important documents to help you produce your review will be your project plan and your diary. You must remember to keep these up to date. You should probably review your project plan at the end of each week. Mark on your plan where you are up to (i.e. which task you are currently doing), and, if it is different, where you should be. Make a note of these in your diary. How often should you do an interim review? Probably every couple of weeks is sufficient, but if you have quiet periods or holidays when not much happens on you project then you may leave it longer than that.

Task 1

You can use a form like the one on page 56 to help you with your interim reviews.

Task 2

You might find it helpful to do your interim reviews in small groups. Fill out the form first, and then print off copies of the form, your diary and your project plan for all the group members. Then discuss how you are doing. Is your review a reasonable reflection of your actual progress?

- Does the group think that what you have entered in question 2 will help you catch up with your plan?

- Does the group have any ideas about how you can solve the problems you have listed in question 3?

- Considering your progress so far, does the group think the rest of your project can be completed on time and to the plan you have created?

Note down the answers to these questions and type them up as part of your review.

Task 3

What happens if your project is taking more or less time than you originally planned? It is very unlikely that your project will go exactly as you planned and each of the tasks in your project plan will take precisely the amount of time you originally allocated to them. Don't panic! In fact, it's difficult to achieve grading criterion D3 ('adapt plans to deal with issues experienced during the project') if this doesn't happen.

If your project is taking much less time than you originally planned, then you can simply revise your project plan (keeping the original as evidence of what happened on the project and for grading criteria P6 and D3). Complete your project early and use the extra time to write up your evidence and do your best to achieve the higher grades.

If your project is taking much longer than planned, you should also revise your plan. Use what you have learned from the first plan (e.g. how much longer some tasks take) to make a better version. You will probably still need to meet the project completion date, so you have a number of choices about how to achieve this:

- Allocate more of your time to working on the project. This may or may not be possible, depending on what other commitments you have.

- Leave out some aspect of the product or system you are producing. Depending on what you plan to produce, you may be able to leave out some feature that is not absolutely essential.

- Get additional help with some aspect of the project that is causing particular problems and delaying you.

Whatever you decide to do to deal with the problem of running late, keep evidence of it, as you will need this when you do your write-up.

3.4   Reviewing the project

In this section we will focus on grading criterion P6 from Unit 3 'ICT Project'.

Learning outcome

Review a project and test the new product or system

Content

Review project plan: appropriateness of project plan; timescales; use of resources; impact of introduction of new system or product

Grading criterion

P6: review a project

Activity 1

Reviewing your project is obviously done at the end of the project, but you need to prepare for your review as you work on the project, by making notes in your diary and completing interim reviews. Your final review can partly consist of a summary of what you entered in your diary. To complete your final review, you need to consider the following questions:

- How did your project plan work out?
  - ◊ Was your plan an accurate list of the tasks you needed to do, or did you discover tasks you had overlooked at the planning stage?
  - ◊ Was the order of tasks correct, or did you end up doing things in a different order?
  - ◊ Did you need to revise your plan? If so, why?
- How did the timing of your project go?
  - ◊ How accurate were your estimates of the lengths of the tasks?
  - ◊ Did you get behind or ahead with your project?
  - ◊ Did you meet the milestone and deadline dates?
  - ◊ Did you need to take action to avoid missing the deadline? If so, what did you do?

- How well did the design of your product or system match what you produced?
  - ◊ Did you need to modify your design? If so, why?
- What resources did you use?
  - ◊ Were you able to accurately predict what resources you would need at the outset? If not, why not?
  - ◊ Did you have access to the resources you needed?
  - ◊ What resources would you like to have had available that were not?
- What problems did you encounter?
  - ◊ What problems or difficulties did you come across while completing the project?
  - ◊ How did you overcome them?
  - ◊ How would you avoid these problems or difficulties next time you do a project?
- What is the impact of your product or system on the users? (To answer these questions you should collect information from your users, perhaps by interview or questionnaire.)
  - ◊ Has your product or system met the users' requirements and expectations?
  - ◊ Do they find your product or system easy to use?
  - ◊ How would they like the product or system to be improved in the future?

There are also some general questions you can try to answer:

- If you did this project again, what would you do differently?
- List three useful things you have learned while doing the project.
- List three mistakes you made while doing the project, and explain how you will avoid them in future.

Interim Review

| Name: |
| Project: |
| Date of review: |
| Task number (from project plan) you should be doing at the moment: |
| Task you are actually doing at the moment: |
| Number of days ahead or behind with your project: |
| Number of weeks to go to the project hand-in date: |

1. If you are ahead or behind with your project, explain what has happened since the last review (or start of the project) to make you ahead or behind.

2. If you are behind with your project, what will you do over the coming weeks to try to catch up?

3. What problems or difficulties have you had (not mentioned above) since your last review? (Your diary may help here.)

4. What has gone well with your project since your last review? (Your diary may help here.)

Marked assignments

Sample assignment

Unit 1 – Using ICT to Present Information

Assignment 1.3: Use of templates to create and review complex documents

Scenario

You are an administrative assistant working in a local company called 'Toytastic!' which specialises in film merchandise. Recently your company has launched a series of action figures for a new blockbuster film being released by NewMedia Film Productions.

The figures below show the sales figures for the four main character figures sold during the first financial quarter (April, May and June). These figures were supplied by the Sales Department on a scruffy handwritten note.

Figure 001 Hero: 30000 units, 35000 units, 40000 units

Figure 002 Villain: 25000 units, 32000 units, 38000 units

Figure 003 Scientist: 17000 units, 27000 units, 25000 units

Figure 004 Soldier: 30000 units, 40000 units, 32000 units

Both the Hero and Villain figures retail for £10.50 each, the Soldier for £10.00 and the Scientist for £9.00.

Task 1 (P4)

Select and use a suitable **pre-defined** word-processing template to present this information to:

a)   Mr Ronald Jones, the Managing Director of Toytastic! – **as a memo**

b)   Miss Sasha Astapkovich, the Head of NewMedia Film Productions – **as a formal business letter.**

NewMedia Film Production's address is 21 Larchwood Drive, Illingham, Worcs., WR12 8DE. (P4)

Task 2 (M2, D1)

Mr Jones has also asked you to produce a mail-merged letter to company shareholders, which displays a simple bar chart showing the income generated for each figure across each of the months in the first financial quarter.

The names and addresses of each of the shareholders should be stored in a database table for the mail merge (see 'Useful data' below for details). The bar chart should be imported from a suitable pre-prepared spreadsheet file. (M2)

The information produced will need to be repeated for each quarter throughout the rest of the year. Create a suitable template for this letter that can be used for the subsequent quarters. (D1)

Task 3 (D1, D2)

(a) An electronic slideshow for this information is also planned for Toytastic!'s annual product review.

A suggested template format for each slide is shown on the right.

Create a suitable template for this slideshow **and** create a suitable slide for the first quarter. (D1)

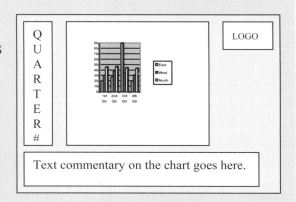

(b) Review the techniques used during the creation of the documents for Tasks 2 and 3(a). Justify the choice of tools used to create each document in terms of the effectiveness of communication to the defined audience. (D2)

Useful data

Shareholder names and addresses:

- Mr W. Patel, 29 Ludhaven Terrace, Ross-on-Wye, Herefordshire
- Mrs J. Plume, 13 Finchcastle Lane, Haresham, Worcestershire
- Miss K. Chinata, Flat 2b, Eli Avenue, Dewhampton, Gloucestershire
- Ms N. Chung, 9 Waterlilly Lane, Hillington, Worcestershire
- Mr J. F. Quesada, Pear Tree Farm, Pauntley, Gloucestershire.

Toytastic! address:

Toytastic!, Units 10–15, Coachchester Trading Estate, Coachchester, Worcestershire, WR12 2MF.

Pass level answers

Wendy Patel – Task 1 (P4)

INTEROFFICE MEMORANDUM

TO: MR RONALD JONES

FROM: WENDY PATEL

SUBJECT: SALES FIGURES

DATE: 30/07/2007

CC: [CLICK **HERE** AND TYPE NAME]

The sales figures for the new film for the first financial quarter (April, may, June) are un this table:

Figure 001 hero	3000 units	35000 units	40000 units
Figure 002 villian	25000 units	32000 units	38000 units
Figure 003 scientist	17000 units	27000 units	25000 units
Figure 004 Soldier	30000 units	40000 units	32000 units

Both the hero and the villain figuires retail for £10.50 each, the soldier for £10.00 and the scientist for £9.00.

Wendy

TOYTASTIC!

Units 10 -15, Colchchester Trading Estate

Coachchester

Worcesestershire

WR12 2MF

July 30, 2007

Miss Sasha Astapokvich
Head of NewMedia Film Productions
21 Larchwood Drive
Illingham
Worces
WR12 8DE

Dear Sir or Madam:

The sales figures for the four main character figures sold during the first financial quarter (April, May and June) are in the table.

Figure 001 hero	3000 units	35000 units	40000 units
Figure 002 villian	25000 units	32000 units	38000 units
Figure 003 scientist	17000 units	27000 units	25000 units
Figure 004 Soldier	30000 units	40000 units	32000 units

Sincerely,

Wendy Patel
Administrative Assistant

Tutor Feedback

Name: Wendy Patel

Task 1 (P4)

You have completed both the tasks but your work needs some improvements before it meets the Pass standard. You have successfully used the built-in memo and letter templates in Microsoft Word but there are a number of errors in both documents which need correcting.

1) The Memo

- You should have removed the text: [Click **here** and type name] under the CC: part of the memo header.

- There are a number of spelling errors in the text of the memo. The month of May must be spelt with a capital 'M'.

- The tone of the memo is very abrupt (remember this is the Managing Director you are talking too!). It would be better to start off with something like 'Please find the sales figures...' and finish off with 'If you require any additional information please let me know' or something similar.

- You have not formatted the table very well. You should have added a row across the top which shows column headings (April, May and June).

- At the end of the memo it would be polite to say 'Regards Wendy', rather than just 'Wendy'

2) The Letter

- Although you have used the template the layout looks a bit messy. The company address at the top is in double line spacing, but the recipient address is in single line. This template is expecting you to add the company address at the bottom of the page, but you have just left this showing the field names. Remember that although traditionally business letters have the sender address at the top, not all templates follow this tradition.

- You have made a number of spelling errors, in both the company address and the recipient address. Remember that with proper names such as Coachchester and Sasha Astapkovich the spell checker will be no help, so you must check them carefully yourself.

- The table suffers from the same problems as the one on your memo.

- The tone of the letter is also very abrupt and it is very brief. You need to at least add some closing comments after the table.

- As the letter template is of US origin it uses the salutation 'Sincerely'. The salutation most commonly used in the UK is 'Yours sincerely'.

You need to make these changes to bring your work up to a Pass standard.

Winston Evans – Task 1 (P4)

Memorandum

To: Mr Ronald Jones

CC:

From: Winston Evans

Date: 17th July 2007

Re: Sales figures for the Action Figures

The table below shows the sales figures as supplied by the Sales Department for the NewMedia action figures:

Figure	Retail Price	Units sold		
		April	May	June
001 – Hero	£10.50	30,000	35,000	40,000
002 – Villain	£10.50	25,000	32,000	38,000
003 – Scientist	£9.00	17,000	27,000	25,000
004 – Soldier	£10.00	30,000	40,000	32,000

Please let me know if you require any additional information.

Regards

Winston

Toytastic!
Units 10 – 15
Coachchester Trading Estate
Worcestershire
WR12 2MF

Toytastic!

July 17, 2007

Miss Sasha Astapkovich
Head of Film Production
NewMedia Film Production
21 Larchwood Drive
Illingham
Worcs.
WR12 8DE

Dear Miss Astapkovich

The table below shows the sales figures in the first quarter of this year for the action figures from your new blockbuster film:

Figure	Retail Price	Units sold		
		April	May	June
001 – Hero	£10.50	30,000	35,000	40,000
002 – Villain	£10.50	25,000	32,000	38,000
003 – Scientist	£9.00	17,000	27,000	25,000
004 – Soldier	£10.00	30,000	40,000	32,000

If you require any additional information please do not hesitate to contact me.

Yours sincerely,

Winston Evans
Administrative Assistant

Toytastic! Film Merchandise

Tutor Feedback

Name: Winston Evans

Task 1 (P4)

You have successfully completed both the tasks and your work meets the Pass standard, well done.

1) The Memo

You have made good use of the template and entered all the fields correctly. You have also added suitable text to the memo. Your table is good and shows you can merge table cells to produce a well formatted clear table with proper column headings.

2) The Letter

This also shows good use of the template with a suitable slogan at the bottom. You have also checked your spelling carefully and have got everything correct.

Merit/Distinction level answers

Sarah Jones – Task 2 (M2, D1)

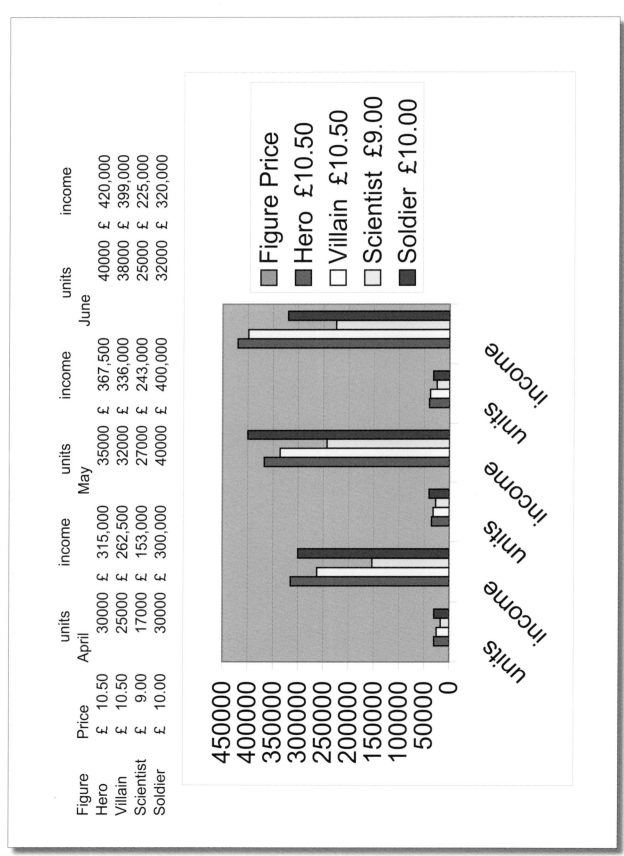

Toytasic!
Units 10 – 15
Coachchester Trading Estate
Worcestershire
WR12 2MF

Toytastic

July 30, 2007

Mr W. Patel

29 Ludhaven Terrace

Ross-on-Wye

Herefordshire

Dear Dear Mr Patel,

The table below shows the sales figures for the first quarter.

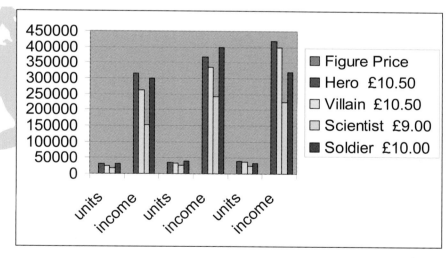

If you want any other information please let me know

Yours sincerely,

Sarah Jones
Admin Assitant

*[Click **here** and type slogan]*

Tutor Feedback

Name: Sarah Jones

Task 2 (M2, D1)

You have completed the mail merge but it needs some improvement before I can award you the Merit criteria. The following issues need addressing:

- There is at least one spelling error in the letter, you need to check it carefully.
- The letter opens: Dear Dear Mr Patel.
- The Template you have used is fine, but you need to add some kind of company slogan at the bottom, you cannot leave the text [Click **here** and type slogan] in the final version of the letter.
- The bar chart needs reformatting. The caption shows you have included a data series for the column title 'Figure price'. This should be removed. You have shown both the units and the income on the chart, I don't think this is a good idea. Shareholders are most likely to be interested in how much money has been made so I think it would be best just to show the income. Charts are meant to display figures in an easy to read format, I don't think your chart achieves this as it is.

You need to resolve these issues if you want to achieve M4. You have not produced a template for this letter so I cannot award D1.

Rasheed Huq – Task 2 (M2, D1)

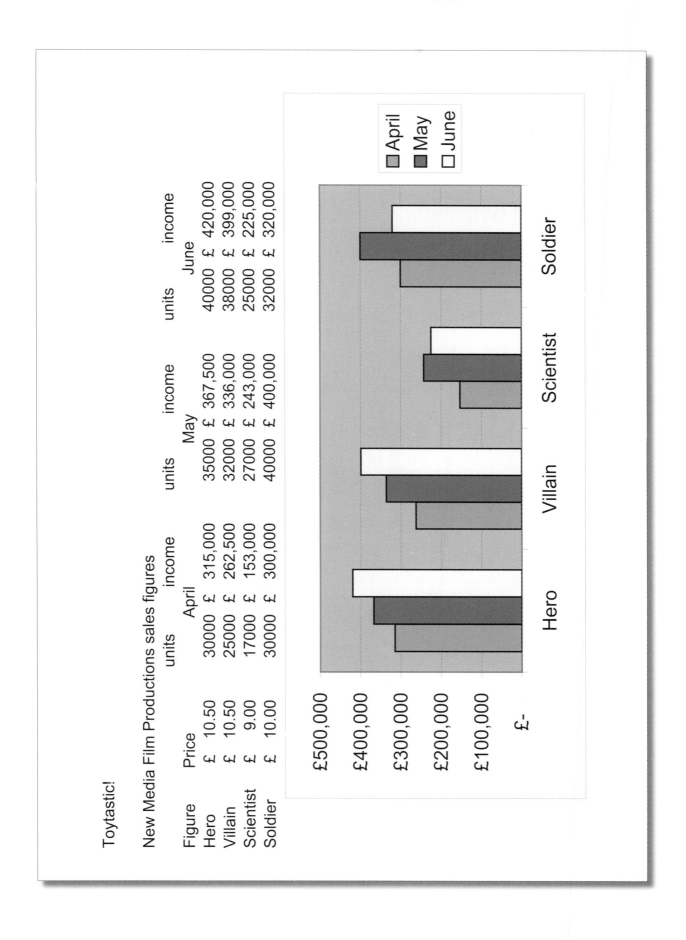

Toytastic!

New Media Film Productions sales figures

Figure	Price	April units	April income	May units	May income	June units	June income
Hero	£ 10.50	30000	£ 315,000	35000	£ 367,500	40000	£ 420,000
Villain	£ 10.50	25000	£ 262,500	32000	£ 336,000	38000	£ 399,000
Scientist	£ 9.00	17000	£ 153,000	27000	£ 243,000	25000	£ 225,000
Soldier	£ 10.00	30000	£ 300,000	40000	£ 400,000	32000	£ 320,000

Toytastic!
Units 10 – 15
Coachchester Trading Estate
Worcestershire
WR12 2MF

Toytastic!

July 30, 2007

Mr W. Patel
29 Ludhaven Terrace
Roos-on-Wye
Herefordshire

Dear Mr Patel,

The chart below shows the income generated in the first quarter of this year for the NewMedia film action figures:

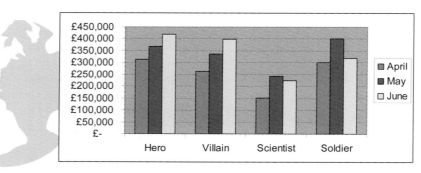

These are really very good results and we hope to do even better next quarter.

Yours sincerely,

Ronald Jones
MD - Toytastic

Toytastic! Film Merchandise

Toytastic!
Units 10 – 15
Coachchester Trading Estate
Worcestershire
WR12 2MF

Toytastic!

July 30, 2007

Mrs J. Plume
13 Finchcastle Lane
Haresham
Worcestershire

Dear Mrs Plume,

The chart below shows the income generated in the first quarter of this year for the NewMedia film action figures:

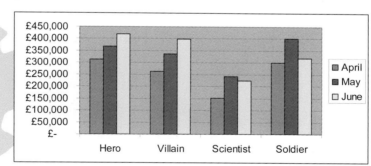

These are really very good results and we hope to do even better next quarter.

Yours sincerely,

Ronald Jones
MD - Toytastic

Toytastic! Film Merchandise

Toytastic!
Units 10 – 15
Coachchester Trading Estate
Worcestershire
WR12 2MF

Toytastic!

July 30, 2007

Miss K. Chinata
Flat 2b
Eli Avenue
Dewhampton
Gloucestershire

Dear Miss Chinata,

The chart below shows the income generated in the first quarter of this year for the NewMedia film action figures:

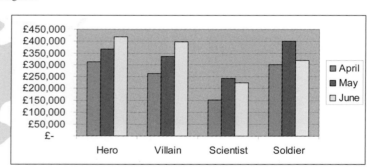

These are really very good results and we hope to do even better next quarter.

Yours sincerely,

Ronald Jones
MD - Toytastic

Toytastic! Film Merchandise

Toytastic!
Units 10 – 15
Coachchester Trading Estate
Worcestershire
WR12 2MF

Toytastic!

July 30, 2007

Ms N. Chung
9 Waterlily Lane
Hillington
Worcestershire

Dear Ms Chung,

The chart below shows the income generated in the first quarter of this year for the NewMedia film action figures:

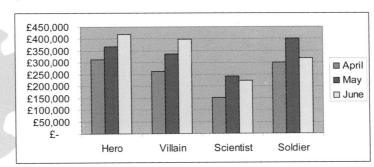

These are really very good results and we hope to do even better next quarter.

Yours sincerely,

Ronald Jones
MD - Toytastic

Toytastic!
Units 10 – 15
Coachchester Trading Estate
Worcestershire
WR12 2MF

Toytastic!

July 30, 2007

Mr J.F. Quesada
Pear Tree Farm
Pauntly
Gloucestershire

Dear Mr Quesada,

The chart below shows the income generated in the first quarter of this year for the NewMedia film action figures:

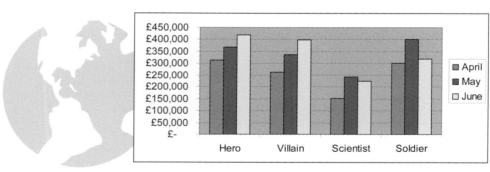

These are really very good results and we hope to do even better next quarter.

Yours sincerely,

Ronald Jones
MD - Toytastic

Toytastic! Film Merchandise

Toytastic!
Units 10 – 15
Coachchester Trading Estate
Worcestershire
WR12 2MF

Toytastic!

July 30, 2007

Mr J.F. Quesada
Pear Tree Farm
Pauntly
Gloucestershire

Dear Mr Quesada,

The chart below shows the income generated in the **[enter quarter]** quarter of this year for the NewMedia film action figures:

[Insert Chart here]

[Enter closing comments here]

Yours sincerely,

Ronald Jones
MD - Toytastic

Toytastic! Film Merchandise

Tutor Feedback

Name: Rasheed Huq

Task 2 (M2, D1)

You have successfully completed the mail merge. Well done. You have used a suitable template for the letter and entered all the names and address data without any errors. You have created and inserted a chart from Excel which clearly shows the income data. The text of the letter is perhaps a little brief but it is adequate for the purpose.

You have also successfully saved a version of the letter as a template and you have added appropriate instructions to the template that can be replaced by the actual text when the template is used.

Distinction level answer

Rasheed Huq – Task 3 (D1, D2)

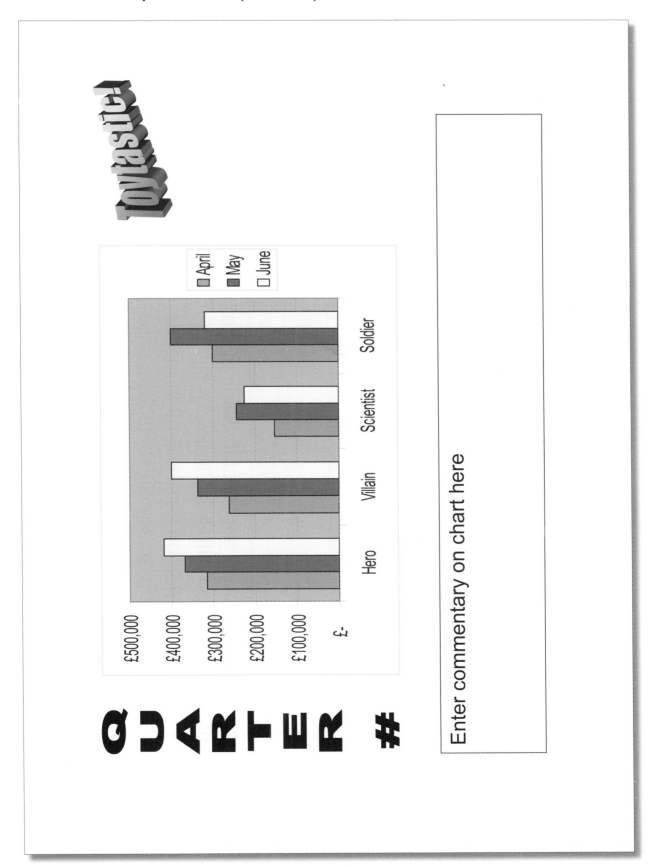

TOYtastic!

QUARTER 1

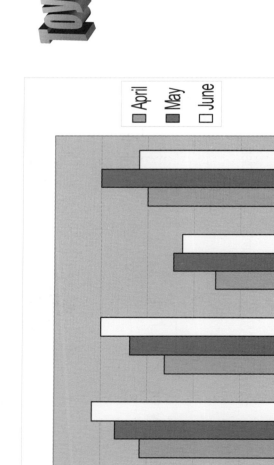

Quarter 1 has been very successful. Sales of the Hero figure have been particularly good with the Villain not far behind. Both these two figures have shown a good increase each month. The Scientist and the Soldier had a drop in their sales in June and sales of the Scientist have been rather disappointing overall. However this is probably due to the role she plays in the film. We are looking forward to continued overall growth in Q2

Assignment 1.3, Task 3b
Name: Rashed Huq

For task 2 I produced a mail merge letter to the shareholders of Toytastic! I used the following techniques:

- **Document template.** I used a template as it gave me a ready made professional layout for the letter. I saved my modified version of the template which means if I need to send out more letters I can use the same template. This saves time and makes sure all the letters look the same which helps promote a professional image for the company. This is important as the shareholders will expect the company to be professional and efficient. I also saved the letter I created as a template so I can use it in future. This will save time and effort when the next quarters results need to be sent out and ensures they are in the same format which promotes a corporate image with the shareholders.

- **Inserting a chart from Excel.** Using a bar chart rather than a table of figures is a good way to present numeric information as it easily allows comparisons to be made between months. Shareholders would be probably more interested in the overall financial performance of the company rather than the detail of individual figures so a bar chart suits this audience well.

- **Mail merge.** I used the mail merge technique to create a set of letters, one to each of the shareholders. This saved time as I did not need to create each letter individually and will also make it easier to send out the letters in future as I have all the people addresses already in a database.

For Task 3 I produced a PowerPoint template and example slide showing the quarterly sales figures. In these slides I used the following features.

- **Word Art.** I used Word Art for the company logo and the vertical 'Quarter 1' text down the side. Word art allows eye catching and colourful 3D text to be created. This is ideal for a logo as it creates something unique and easily recognisable. People at the annual product review will expect to see the company logo used consistently on all documentation as this enhances the corporate image.

- **Large font text.** For the text describing the chart on the slide I used a large font size (size 20). This will make the size easy to read when it is projected to the audience at the annual product review which is likely to take place in a large meeting room, so some people may be some distance form the projector screen.

- **Inserting a chart from Excel.** As in the letter, using a chart is a good way to represent financial information. People at the product review will probably be interested in the overall trends in the sales of the figures and this can be easily seen on a chart.

- **Creation of a template.** I have created a template for all the other slides which will be used at the product review for showing the sales figures of other products. Using a template will make sure all the slides have a similar layout which will demonstrate to the audience that Toytasic! is a professional company with a strong corporate image.

Tutor Feedback

Name: Rasheed Huq

Task 3 (D1, D2)

You have successfully created a slide for the annual product review and also created a template slide. The slide in well laid out following the suggested format. The template is also fine although you could have added slide numbers to improve it further. This along with the letter template you produced for task 2 covers the D1 grading criteria.

You have also written a good justification of the features you have used. You have properly related the use of these features to the target audiences and identified how they help communicate more effectively. This covers D2.

Overall you have demonstrated your skills in using Word, Excel and PowerPoint and also shown a good understand of the requirements of a particular audience. Well done.